PUF

Edito

So Pete's German trip with the school was off. O.K., then, he'd put the angry headmaster and the lost holiday right out of his mind and do something else. Why, it was almost a piece of luck, giving him a chance to do the two things he'd always wanted – go to a football match, and visit his quiet, hard-to-know father who was always on building schemes for weeks at a time, and was so quiet when he came home that he hardly seemed to matter.

Pete saw himself walking up the great new road his father was building on the remote island of Kell. 'Hello, Dad,' he'd say, and the tall man at the centre of the group would turn and smile slowly, and say, 'Why, it's our Pete!' – but that was only the dream, and Pete had a lot to go through, including being beaten up by hoodlums and sleeping rough in a railway carriage with a family of drop-outs, before the long journey of discovering his father was even begun.

It was worth it in the end though, with the new warm, glowing feeling of companionship, and the proud realization later on that his father was one of life's quiet heroes, a man to be really proud of.

This book is the successor to Alison Morgan's very successful *Fish*, which was serialized on BBC television and is also published in Puffin.

In 1973, *Pete* was the first children's book to receive a Welsh Arts Council Literary Award.

Alison Morgan

PETE

PUFFIN BOOKS

Puffin Books, Penguin Books Ltd, Harmondsworth, Middlesex, England
Penguin Books Australia Ltd, Ringwood, Victoria, Australia
Penguin Books Canada Ltd,
41 Steelcase Road West, Markham, Ontario, Canada
Penguin Books (N.Z.) Ltd,
182-190 Wairau Road, Auckland 10, New Zealand

First published by Chatto & Windus 1972
Published in Puffin Books 1975

Made and printed in Great Britain
by Hazell Watson & Viney Ltd
Aylesbury, Bucks
Set in Intertype Plantin

To Geoffrey

Chapter 1

'I HEAR Tom's going on the school trip, then,' said Sam, settling himself at his sister's table and ladling peas and potatoes on to his plate.

'What trip's that, then?' asked Mrs Jenkins. 'You've never said nothing about it, Pete. Have you got gravy, Sam? Pass your uncle the gravy, Pete, there's a good boy.'

'There wasn't nothing to tell,' said Pete, pushing the gravy jug across. His Uncle Sam was the village policeman and lived just across the road. He was a bachelor, and often came over to his sister's for a meal, and always for Sunday dinner. Pete's father worked for an engineering firm, and was away for long spells building motorways and living on a works site that moved around Britain in a clutter of shabby caravans and vast earth-moving machines. Every six weeks or so he would come home and sit, silent and sinewy, in the sagging armchair, while the village talk flowed back and forth between Mrs Jenkins, and Sam, and Pete. Then, after a couple of days, Mrs Jenkins would pack up his clean linen and put a large home-made pie in his haversack, and he would stow them in the back of the battered A.30, and go.

'School trip to Germany,' said Sam. 'Or so Tom's father was saying. Isn't that right, Pete?'

'Yeah,' said Pete. 'That's right.'

'First I've heard about it,' said Mrs Jenkins. 'They go everywhere nowadays, children do.'

'Not like when we were kids,' said Sam. 'Thought you

might be going, Pete. You're in the same form as Tom, aren't you?'

'Yeah,' said Pete. 'But I'm not going.'

'Why not?' asked his mother.

'You wouldn't let me,' said Pete. He stuffed in a huge mouthful of potato.

'You never asked,' said his mother. 'Why, I didn't even know there was a trip till Uncle Sam mentioned it just now.'

'Do you know what it costs, then?' demanded Pete.

'No, but you might have told me.'

'If you knew how much it cost you wouldn't let me go.' Pete stretched across and helped himself to more vegetables.

'Peter, leave some for your uncle. Goodness, I've never seen a boy eat potatoes the way you do. How much does it cost, then? After all, we might be able to find it.'

'You wouldn't let me go to the Cardiff City match against Sheffield Wednesday and that wouldn't have cost a quarter as much, I bet.'

'Thirty-five pounds, Tom's dad said,' Sam remarked. 'Pretty reasonable he thought, considering it was for a fortnight, and all in. Trips to places of interest and that, once you got there.'

'It's a lot of money, though, Sam.'

'Forget it,' said Pete. 'I don't want to go.' He collected up the empty plates and, tilting his chair so that he could reach, slid them on to the draining-board across the narrow kitchen.

'Now, Pete,' said his mother, 'how often have I told you not to do that, but to get up properly and carry them over. One of these days there'll be a nasty crash, and then you'll be sorry.' She cut into the fruit pie. 'These are your blackcurrants, Sam, the ones you brought over last night.'

'Oh, aye,' said Sam. 'Got a good crop this year.' He ate deliberately, and Pete had finished his helping before Sam spoke again. 'About that school trip,' he said. 'It seems a shame our Pete can't go, if all the other boys is going.'

'Yes, well,' said Mrs Jenkins, 'indeed I don't know why Pete never told me nothing about it till now. I know it's a lot of money, but it's a wonderful opportunity to see the world. It would help with his exams, I shouldn't wonder. We'll have to think about it.'

Pete got up. 'I shouldn't worry if I were you,' he said. 'I'd sooner go to a football match any day.'

'Don't talk so foolish,' said Sam. 'Maybe you'll never get another chance like this to travel and see all the famous sights of Europe.'

'Tramping round old castles,' said Pete, 'and lots of kids being sick on the boat. Can I go now, Mum?'

'Yes, be off with you. And another time, you let me be judge of whether we can afford something or not.'

Pete went out of the back door and stood in the little square of garden, considering what to do. His mother and Uncle Sam probably thought he was rushing off to meet Tom to get up to something together, because grown-ups always expected you to go on doing the same things, and wanting to be with the same people. Just because Pete and Tom had started at the village school the same term, and shared a desk all through their primary school life, and gone off together on the school bus to the secondary school at the same time, and taught each other football, and shared secret jokes and secret pranks all the twelve years of their lives, people like Uncle Sam seemed to take it for granted that it would always be like that. Well, Tom was all right, and maybe they would always be good friends, just like Uncle Sam and Tom's father were good friends, but that didn't mean they were Siamese twins. There were other boys in the world besides Tom – even girls; and some things that Tom liked doing that did not interest Pete, like stamp-collecting, and some things that Pete liked doing best by himself, like bird-watching. Tom wasn't patient enough; he liked to talk, and swish about in the woods with a long stick, or skim stones across the water, and that way you never saw anything.

Pete turned back in through the door, collected a dog-eared

I-Spy Birds booklet off the top of the television, hunted around till he found a stub of pencil, put them both in his trouser pocket and made his way quietly across the fields behind the houses, to the stream.

All the fields between the stream and the main road to town belonged to Tom's father, John Thomas, who lived at Tygwyn, a little way out of the main village. He was the largest landowner in the district, and a County Councillor, and though Tom was the second youngest in a family of five, there did not seem to be any difficulty in finding the money for him to go on the school trip. And he had been to a football match. Mrs Thomas's sister lived near Cardiff, and her youngest boy, Alan, was just a year older than Tom. Tom was always talking about Alan, and what he did and what he said and what a good footballer he was, even before that match. Afterwards, having spent the day with him and watched Cardiff City playing at Ninian Park, he talked about him even more. Pete, who had never met Alan, began to dislike him heartily. To be fair, Mr Thomas had asked Pete to go with them, but Pete had gone down with measles the day before, so Tom's younger brother, Gary, had taken *his* friend, Jimmy Price, instead. Gary and Jimmy were only ten, and had not even played in the village team themselves, yet. Then, when two months later there was a chance of getting a seat on an excursion coach to Cardiff to see their big match against Sheffield Wednesday, his mother had told Pete it would cost too much and he wasn't old enough to join in a football crowd on his own. And now she seemed quite prepared to fork out thirty-five pounds to send him all the way to Germany.

Pete kicked crossly at a piece of brushwood in his path. He had to follow along by the hedge because, it being June, many of the fields were down for hay. Disturbed by the sudden rustle, a wren flitted noiselessly along ahead of him, then burst into strident song, the little upright brown tail flicking like a trigger. Pete peered into the hedge to see if he could find the nest, but the hawthorn grew too thick; he picked some of the bright tips of the shoots, green edged with red, and nibbled at them between his front teeth. The sky was very blue, and when he got to the corner of the field beside the stream he flung himself on his back and stared up into space, trying to pick out the speck he knew must be there somewhere, like a minute transistor radio, flooding the air with lark song. It was already on its way down by the time he was able to focus on it; even so, with nothing but the cloudless sky for perspective, he could fool himself that it was a vast eagle hovering thousands of feet up, or a little midge trampolining on the breeze a few inches from his nose; until suddenly, with a spreading of wings, it took form as a very ordinary little brown bird, and disappeared into the long grass twenty yards away.

Pete was tempted to go and look for the lark's nest, but the meadow was almost ready for cutting, and in full view from Tygwyn. He decided he had better not, so slipped under the barbed-wire strand that fenced the meadow from the stream, and stood in the dappled shadow among the alders at the water's edge. Here the ground was boggy, even in June, and Pete stepped from tussock to tussock to avoid the peaty mud, churned up by cows coming down to drink before the field had been shut up for hay. A few marsh marigolds were in flower, but sparingly in the shade of the alders, and a couple of dragonflies alternately darted and rested, the small kind with bright blue bodies, kingfisher blue, and transparent wings. Upstream, as Pete knew, the ground was firmer, and a little spit of dry shingle ran out into the water. Here he sat down, hugging his knees.

He knew that if he sat still for a while, the silent trees about him would begin to take life; first, maybe, a solitary tit chirring softly but insistently at the invader, then a willow warbler flitting about the branches, apparently unperturbed by a human presence, but no doubt keeping a wary eye on him all the same, then a robin, cocking his head with friendly effrontery; then one would be aware of birds everywhere, hopping in the further branches, preening just out of the corner of one's eye, foraging in the leaves behind one's unturned head. If he sat long enough, like a human log, he could move, immobile, into another world as surely as if he had stepped into a time-machine or a space-rocket, a world of slugs and midges and dragonflies and innumerable preoccupied birds, and even, eventually, of rabbits and squirrels and bright inquisitive wood-mice – but that took patience, more than even Pete was master of.

Tom was useless for this kind of voyage. If you told him that by walking fifteen miles along the banks of the stream he would see a dipper or a kingfisher, he would have done it willingly, but if you told him he could see the same birds sitting silently in one place for ten minutes, he could not have done it to save his life.

Yet Tom was a lot of fun. Maybe a fortnight in Germany would be quite something, with Tom as a companion. But then, Tom had made a lot of new friends since they had gone to the big secondary school; Pete had made some friends, too, but his friends were not going on the trip. Tom's friends were. Would he find himself a hanger-on, dependent on Tom's good nature not to leave him out of the fun? They would probably have more pocket-money to spend than him. By the time his mum and Uncle Sam had raised the necessary thirty-five pounds there would not be much left for Pete to spend on Coke and souvenirs. Anyhow, if they were going to let him have that great sum of money, why shouldn't he be allowed to spend it on what he really wanted to do – go to football matches? He wished he lived near a town like Tom's cousin Alan, and could take himself to a football match whenever he wanted to.

Angrily, he kicked a spray of pebbles into the water, and at once he was aware of a sudden stillness. While he had been brooding on his frustrations, the very world he had wanted to invade had come to life around him; now, with his sudden movement, it had melted instantly away. There was not a bird to be seen.

He got up, fed up with the whole afternoon. What did he want with watching other creatures living their lives? Why couldn't he do exciting things himself?

'Such as what?' he asked himself. Proper old dump, this place was. Talk about the joys of living in the country. What was an able-bodied thirteen-year-old boy meant to do with himself on a long Sunday afternoon in a small village in the heart of the country? He had not even got any brothers or sisters of his own, and there were precious few other children of his age, except Tom.

He supposed he might as well go and see Tom, and so he made his way back downstream to where the lane came down from Tygwyn and crossed the stream by a small bridge and wound away up over the hills on the farther side. He was just about to climb over the fence on to the road, when he heard the sound of a pony's hooves, and round the corner came Gary, Tom's younger brother, casually astride the farm pony.

'Hiya, Pete,' said Gary, and clattered over the bridge and disappeared round the next bend.

'Hiya,' said Pete. Normally, Gary, being a good bit younger, would have waited, hopefully, for Pete to notice him first, but the pony made a difference. He was probably on his way up to the open hillside to help his father round up the sheep, for they had grazing rights there. It was a common Sunday afternoon occupation for the hill-farmers, whose chapel traditions were still strong enough to make them feel uncomfortable about ploughing or hedging on a Sunday; but shepherding, with its hallowed places in the pages of the Bible, was different. Pete had been up sometimes with the Thomas family and stood, feet damp in peat-stained plimsolls, or relaxed on the broad warm back of the old pony, watching the dogs streak off through the singing grasses to bring the sheep from here, from there, grazing in the crinkles of the moor, up in orderly little columns along the narrow sheep tracks till they formed a noisy, eddying pool around the farmer and his boys.

Just then, Pete heard the Land-rover approaching down the lane. Maybe if he had climbed the fence and stood in the road looking hopeful, they would have picked him up and taken him with them, but he found himself, instead, peering deliberately down at the stream, as though to give the impression that he was absorbed in an important activity of his own. He just had time to catch a glimpse of Tom sitting in the Land-rover with his father and older brother, before it was gone.

So there it was. If you were a farmer's son and living in the country, there was nearly always a useful job for you to do. Pete had to carry the coals for his mother, and do a few dreary jobs around the garden, but the one task he really fancied was using the rotary mower to cut the grass; but this was the prerogative of Uncle Sam. Jimmy Price was a farmer's boy as well. He was the oldest so no doubt, although he was only ten, he would be busy this quiet Sunday afternoon with some responsible job on the farm. Perhaps Fish was around somewhere? Fish was only ten, too, and seemed small and young for that, but he would be better than nothing. Pete climbed over by the bridge and walked, not up the lane leading to Tygwyn, but straight along the short cut that followed the course of the stream and led eventually back into the main village. During the day-time, if there was no school, boys at a loose end tended to congregate near the village shop, but in the evenings and on Sundays, when the shop was closed, they would lean on the parapet of the bridge down at the bottom end of the village. Nearly all the houses were clustered in little groups on the nearer side but the school and the church, and one farm, were over the other side.

Today the only people on the bridge were three old men, breaking long intervals of silence with scraps of leisured chat while they waited for the pub to open. Pete could not stand about with them, so he walked slowly up the village street. One family was climbing into their car to visit relatives and a couple of housewives sat in their respective gardens knitting and talking to each other across the narrow roadway, but those with larger households were still indoors, clearing up or recovering from the efforts of Sunday dinner. The postman was trimming his hedge, and the clink of fork on stone or trundling sound of a laden wheelbarrow suggested that a few of the men were spending Sunday afternoon in their back gardens. But of anybody young and looking for something to do, there was no sign.

With flagging interest, Pete strolled through the village, past his own silent house, and on up to the cross-roads where, to get to Fish's house, he turned left. He was too old to knock at the cottage door and ask, like a little boy, if Fish could come and play, but there was no harm in hanging about the road near by, as though by chance, and getting into conversation with Fish if he were anywhere to be seen. He was not, though; only his father, Mr Barnes, stood in the open doorway lighting his pipe. The Barneses were comparative newcomers to the village, and Mr Barnes was a strange, unfriendly sort of man. Now he glanced with morose lack of interest at Pete, and went on lighting his pipe.

Pete did not feel sufficiently encouraged by this to ask where Fish was, so he walked on up the road, because he felt silly just turning round in his tracks at the sight of Mr Barnes, whom he had plainly not come to see. The steep lane ended at the Rhos, Jimmy Price's farm. Here the place had a deserted air; the dogs barked behind an outhouse door, and the shed where the van was kept stood empty. The Prices, too, had gone out for the day. Rather than walk back past The Ferns, Fish's cottage, Pete cut across the fields to the main road, coming out above the cross-roads, on the side nearest the market town, Aberafon. He had just started to plod dispiritedly back down into the village when a motorbike came stuttering up the hill towards him.

As the machine passed, the rider turned his head, gave a half-wave, and braked to a stop.

The rider looked over his shoulder. 'Hi, Pete,' he said.

'Hi, Sid,' said Pete. He walked back up and stood alongside the machine. 'I didn't know you'd got a bike,' he said.

Sid pulled the old scarf from the lower part of his face and grinned. 'I've only had her a week,' he said. 'Somebody brought her into the garage, and the boss said I could have her for a tenner.' Sid was a cousin of Pete's and lived, along with a ramshackle collection of Pete's father's relations, up in the mountain hamlet of Llandewi-fach, across the river from the village. Pete's mother disapproved of a good deal of their goings-on, and from time to time told Pete that he need not think he was going to leave school as soon as he was fifteen and work in a garage, like his cousin Sid.

'She goes a treat,' Sid said proudly.

'For a week,' said Pete.

'Cheeky devil,' said Sid. ' 'Course she's not new, and maybe for someone who didn't know nothing about engines she might give a bit of trouble. But when you've worked in a garage for a bit, it helps. You know the kind of things to look for.'

'She didn't sound too good coming up that hill,' said Pete. It rankled a little that dull Sid Jenkins should come by like a lord on his motorbike and find him wandering along the road bored and companionless.

'Try her,' said Sid. He slapped the worn pillion seat.

'What do you think I am? A member of the suicide squad or something?' Pete made his voice sound off-hand, but his eyes brightened.

'Come on. Come into Aberafon for a run. I'm meeting some of the boys there.' Pete took a turn around the bike, pretending to examine it with a connoisseur's eye. The dangling L-plates caught his eye.

'You can't take passengers if you're a learner,' he objected. A ride into Aberafon would be fine, but he knew he could not rely on Sid to bring him back before he was missed at home.

'On Sunday afternoon?' asked Sid. 'Don't tell me Uncle Sam isn't sleeping off his Sunday dinner in your mum's kitchen.' Pete still hesitated. He was bored, and a lift on the bike would be fun, but he did not want to be obliged to Sid, and he did not altogether trust him. All the same . . .

'Are you coming or aren't you?' demanded Sid. 'Look, if anyone did stop us, you could always say you didn't know I was a learner. You don't need to have noticed the plates, and anyway it's me they'll blame, not you.' A car was passing, and Sid paused a minute, then when it was safely out of sight he slipped off the L-plates. 'That satisfy you?' he asked. 'Come on; hop on.'

'How am I going to get home then?' asked Pete, but he was already swinging a leg over the seat.

'I've got to go past your place to get home myself, haven't I?' demanded Sid.

'Yes, I know that, but how long are you staying in town?'

'Oh, stop fussing. I'll see you get home all right.' Sid twisted the throttle and the roar of the engine made further talk impossible. Pete felt a surge of excitement as he laid his hands on Sid's leather jacket – lightly, so that Sid wouldn't think he was hanging on for dear life, but tensed ready to grip if need arose. The swerve round the first corner gave him a sudden fright, and he clutched involuntarily.

'Lean with me,' Sid shouted into the wind. Pete could hear the grin in his voice. 'Like as you were on a push-bike.' That was only sensible, but on a push-bike you had command of your own handlebars and your own pedals – and anyway you did not go so fast.

After a couple of miles, though, Pete began to get the feel of the movement, and then it was sheer delight. He and Sid and the motor-bike swept up the hills and leaned into the corners like a single super-creature, as casually as Gary on his hairy pony.

Pete would have ridden to Cardiff or London or Timbuctoo. The half-dozen miles to Aberafon were soon over, and Sid coasted in along the deserted main street and drew up where a couple of youths were leaning against a wall by the telephone kiosk. Pete tried to step off with an accustomed air, but found it hard work not to stagger when the pavement failed to lean and give with his weight. Luckily no one seemed to notice.

'Hi,' said the youths to Sid. Pete knew them vaguely by sight, but not well; they had all left school a couple of terms after he had gone there. 'Who's your passenger?' one of them asked, and Sid explained that he had been giving his cousin a ride.

'You're asking for trouble,' the other youth said briefly. 'There's a copper about. I just seen one go by a few minutes ago.'

'Well, I'm not taking anyone now, am I?' said Sid.

Pete wondered what they were going to do now they had got here, but none of the others seemed in any hurry to do anything. They stood around and talked about people and places that Pete knew nothing of, with long pauses between each remark. One of the boys lit a cigarette, the other drummed a rhythm on the kiosk window-pane with his finger-nails, while Sid fiddled with his machine. Every now and then one of them would say, 'What shall we do then?' and nobody answered. After a time a group of four girls appeared at the end of the street and as they drew near they began laughing and talking among themselves so loudly that they seemed scarcely to notice the youths, though Pete gathered from a comment made by one of the boys when they first came into view that they knew one another quite well. The girls just said hullo as they passed and then stopped some twenty yards on down the road, on the opposite side, by a vending machine. They did not buy anything, just stood there laughing until the boy with the cigarette suddenly decided he wanted a hot drink from the machine. 'Coming, Sid?' he said. The other youth said he thought he might as well have one, too. Nobody asked Pete, and he had not got any money with him. He stayed where he was, by the bike, waiting for them to come back, but they did not seem in any hurry to do that. It appeared the girls wanted drinks, too. Eventually they all strolled on up the road together.

Pete did not know what to do. He could not go running after them saying, 'Hey, what about me?' but he did not fancy hanging about forlornly all afternoon waiting for Sid to decide to go home.

'Hi, Sid,' he shouted, not too loud. 'What time are you likely to be starting home?' That sounded fairly unconcerned. Sid apparently did not hear him, but one of the girls did. 'What's that little boy want, then?' he heard her say, and Sid turned reluctantly round.

'What time will you be going home?' Pete shouted again. He felt very silly.

'Oh, shouldn't think I'll be more than half an hour,' Sid replied. 'Hang around and I'll be back.'

'Don't be daft, the pubs won't even have opened by then,' Pete heard one of the girls say, and Sid shrugged as if to say, 'Well, he'll just have to wait then.' Pete looked at the motor-bike longingly. What fun it would be to get on and zoom off up the road past them, waving airily to Sid as he went by.

Although he knew it was an impossibility, Pete put his hands on the handlebars and leaned the bike sideways, testing its weight, then raised the support and tried again. This time the inert heaviness of the machine nearly pulled him over into the road on top of it. He hastily put the support back in place and moved away up the pavement, whistling in an unconcerned way as a stray car passed by along the deserted street.

The car gave him an idea. There was no need to hang about forlornly waiting for Sid to decide to go home; he would start along the road, and almost certainly be able to get a lift. If he didn't Sid would have to pass him in the long run, so he would be no later home than if he waited here. He started walking, then paused, in two minds what to do. Would Sid go hunting around the town for him when he got back and found no obedient Pete waiting by the bike? It would serve him right for landing him in this position, but on the other hand he might never offer Pete another ride on the bike, and even go so far as to sail past him on the road if he failed to hitch a lift earlier. A couple of young mothers with a pram and a clutch of toddlers were slowly making their way up the street and Pete decided to make off.

He started walking homeward, but as soon as he rounded the bend he saw Sid and his group still dawdling along the road not very far ahead. Should he just walk past, casually telling Sid what he was doing? He did not feel like doing that, so slipped off down a side alley. He knew the town well, from many school dinner-hours spent mooching about with his friends, and he decided to cut through to the back road which would lead him on to the homeward route again on the outskirts of the town.

Then he suddenly saw Vince. Vince had recently become rather a friend of Pete's. They sat together in class and kicked a football around in the same group during breaks, but Pete did not see much of him in the dinner-hour because, being a town boy, Vince went home for his dinner. Vince was leaning against a wall at the corner where the alley joined a short street and almost immediately before the street itself opened on to the back road. The back road was not a very busy place, but it had a few shops and terraced houses and quite a bit of through traffic used it as a by-pass. The side street where Vince was standing was little more than a yard. Just beyond Vince was a small tobacconist's, and beyond that a builder's yard ran the remaining length of the street and blocked off the end, and on the opposite side were the blank windowless back walls of shops and offices. The smaller boys at school often used the place as a base for games of cops and robbers or cowboys and Indians. But for the fact that Pete and his class-mates had gone a bit beyond that sort of game, he would have guessed that was what Vince was doing now, because though he was apparently alone, he had a purposeful, watchful look about him.

He was gazing intently the other way – towards the main road – when Pete first noticed him, so Pete slid quietly to the other side of the alley, where the curve of the wall hid him from Vince until he was a few yards away. Then he jumped into view, giving a piercing whistle.

If he had hoped to make Vince jump, he was not disappointed. The effect was remarkable. Vince whipped round and stood a second transfixed like a frightened rabbit. For a moment Pete thought he was going to bolt, but then he relaxed.

'Hi, Vince,' said Pete, cheerfully. Suddenly he had found a friend. 'What are you doing here?'

'Nothing special.' Vince still looked confused. After a pause he said, 'What are you doing?' It was a fair question. Vince, after all, did live in town.

Pete told him about his frustrating afternoon, glad at last to have found someone of his own age to talk to, but Vince seemed restless. He kept glancing about him, now down towards the main road, now up the alley behind them, now along the deserted yard. Pete broke off in the middle of his tale.

'What's the matter with you?' he demanded. 'Are you looking for someone?'

'No,' said Vince. 'No, not really.' Pete looked at him in sceptical silence. 'Well,' added Vince, 'I am in a way. I suppose.' He suddenly laid a nervous hand on Pete's arm. 'Hush a minute!'

Now they could hear voices somewhere along the back road.

'See who it is,' whispered Vince. 'But don't let them see you.'

'Why not?' asked Pete.

'I'll tell you afterwards. Go on!'

'Why can't you go yourself?'

'Because I've got to guard the alley, too. Now quick!'

Pete could not think what all the mystery was about, but Vince was a lot more fun to be with than Sid, or no one. He ran softly down to the corner and flattened himself against the wall, cowboy-style, before peering round the corner. Sid's group, having cut through another side street, were now sauntering slowly towards him. Pete certainly did not want to be caught out spying on *them,* so he turned back to pass the information on to Vince. To his surprise, Vince had been joined by two other boys who had apparently sprung from nowhere. They seemed to have come from the direction of the tobacconist's, but the only way into the cul-de-sac was over the paling from the builder's yard. One of the boys was Vince's older brother, usually known as Curly, and the other was his friend Steve.

'What's Pete doing here?' Curly asked Vince suspiciously.

'I just happened along,' said Pete.

'That's right,' said Vince, anxiously. 'He's been helping me keep a look-out. Who was that down there?' Pete told him.

'Coming this way?' asked Curly. Pete said they were. 'Come on, then,' went on Curly. 'We'll nip up the alley, and go down to the river.' He turned and walked rapidly up the alley-way, followed by Steve. They both had their hands thrust into bulging anorak pockets. Vince and Pete scurried after them.

'What's it all about?' asked Pete.

'You'll see when we get there,' said Vince. 'Only you must promise not to split,' he added as an afterthought.

''Course not,' said Pete automatically, but the remark kept him wondering. 'Who to, anyway?' But Vince just said, 'Ssh,' as they reached the shopping street again, crossed it and followed it down to the bridge, which lay on the further edge of the town. The river here had never been turned into a centre of interest. Some tumbledown old warehouses huddled along one bank, and on the other lay a quiet meadow. Some way downstream a fisherman stood thigh deep in the water, his back to a stretch of shingle still littered with the odd broken pram or worn-out tyres brought down in the winter floods, and some children played on the far bank a good way beyond him. Immediately by the bridge there was no one, and the boys climbed on to the low parapet and dropped to the grass below. Curly led the way down to the first archway – in winter-time the tawny waters rushed through here, but now it was just shingle and dry mud with the occasional clump of dusty nettles. Curly leant against the arch, and looked at Pete.

'Does he know what we've been up to?' he asked Vince.

'I don't know,' said Vince. 'Not unless he's guessed.'

'Guessed what?' asked Pete, a little uncomfortably.

'Yeah, well,' said Curly. He did not seem to know how to go on. 'Have a Crunchie,' he said suddenly, and produced an assortment of sweets from his pockets. 'Come on, Steve; open up.'

'I suppose it's all right – about him, I mean,' said Steve, doubtfully, pulling some packets of cigarettes and some ice-lollies from his pockets. 'You two kids will have to share the lolly; I only got three.'

'My job was much more dangerous than yours,' began Vince, but Steve cut him short.

'Standing on a street corner? There's no law against that.'

A kind of cold trickling feeling was starting somewhere at the back of Pete's neck and running down to his toes and finger-tips. It was dank enough under the bridge, but that wasn't the cause. He had not spoken since they left the alley, and now it was too late to ask questions, too late even to draw back. Mechanically, he unwrapped the Crunchie, and took a large bite. The chocolate was comforting, and the shivers passed. His first thoughts – 'Oh, but that's stealing!' and 'I don't want to have anything to do with it,' and even, simply, 'What if we're found out?' – suddenly seemed better unsaid. He took another mouthful, swallowed it in a leisurely manner, and then said, coolly, 'How did you get in?'

The other boys had been watching him uncomfortably, cornerways, as they parcelled out the spoils, but now they relaxed.

Curly said, 'You won't tell anyone at all, will you? Grown-ups, of course, but I mean not any other boys, either.'

' 'Course not.'

'Not even people like Tom?' said Vince, carefully. He knew Pete better than the other two did.

'No,' said Pete. No, this was something he could never tell Tom.

'Good,' said Steve. He opened a packet of cigarettes and handed them round. Curly and Vince each took one in a matter-of-fact manner, so Pete did, too. 'Your first fag?' asked Steve, glancing at him curiously.

'Nuh,' said Pete. In a sense it wasn't. Now and again a boy would smuggle a cigarette into school, and it would be passed from hand to hand for furtive puffs behind the boys' toilets, but it was the first time he had had a whole one all to himself. Steve struck a match – Pete noticed the matchbox was quite new, so presumably he had taken it along with the other things – and he hoped he made a confident business of getting his cigarette alight.

'It's easy getting into that place,' said Curly.

'Dead easy,' said Steve.

'You couldn't call it breaking and entering,' Curly went on. 'It's more like just entering. The lock don't fasten properly. You just give the door a good push, and a sort of rattle, and the two doors swing open together.'

'Did you shut them again properly after you?' asked Vince.

' 'Course,' said Curly.

'Have you done it often before?' asked Pete.

'Once or twice, maybe,' said Curly vaguely. 'We don't take a lot. You can't call it stealing.'

'He's never even noticed yet,' said Steve.

'I don't reckon old Bongo would notice if you pinched half the shop,' remarked Curly. 'Silly old fool.'

Vince glanced sharply at Pete's expression. 'It's not as if they ever took money,' he said defensively, though Pete had not spoken. 'Only a few sweets and a couple of packets of fags. He'd never miss them.' Pete saw Curly give Steve an odd look, but Steve seemed not to notice.

'It's not a bad idea, having an extra look-out,' he said thoughtfully. 'So long as it's someone you can trust. There's a lot of ways you got to watch. You often in town on a Sunday?'

Pete shook his head. He was partly relieved, partly disappointed. 'I just happened to get a lift in today with my cousin Sid,' he said. 'On his motorbike,' he added, with a trace of pride. He suddenly looked at his cigarette in one hand and his Crunchie in the other. The other three boys seemed to be munching and puffing alternately without any ill effects, but Pete became aware that he would have to choose between the Crunchie and the fag, and he very much preferred the Crunchie. In fact, he decided, half a cigarette was about twice as much smoking as he cared to undertake at any one time.

'Kids' stuff!' he remembered Jones, the soccer captain, saying one day when he caught a gang of them passing a fag-end around. He had looked at Pete, an earnest contender for the Colts XI. 'You'll never make a footballer creeping around the pitch with a smoker's cough,' he had added caustically.

Pete held his half-smoked cigarette out. 'Anyone want it? I'm trying to give it up, really,' he remarked manfully.

Steve gave a short laugh. 'Chuck it away then. We're not that short,' he commented, holding up another unopened packet.

Pete hesitated a moment, then flipped it into the river. Suddenly in his mind he saw old Bongo muddling along in his murky little shop, trying to eke a living out of kids' pocket-money, and a wave of disgust flooded through him like a pain.

'I must go,' he said abruptly. 'I don't want to miss my lift home with Sid.'

'Take your share then before you go,' said Curly.

'I've had enough, ta,' said Pete. 'It's you who got the stuff, not me. I just happened to come along.'

'You're in it like the rest of us, and you take your share,' said Steve, roughly. He and Curly laid out the haul upon the shingle and proceeded to divide it. The system seemed to be that the two bigger boys kept the cigarettes, and the sweets were divided into three equal portions, one for Steve, one for Curly, and one to be shared between Vince and Pete. Vince protested at this arrangement, but Curly explained that was how it was arranged beforehand and if Vince had brought Pete in afterwards that was his affair.

'I don't want any,' Pete said again, but the big boys said he must.

'If ever we're found out,' said Curly, 'we're all in it together.'

'Of course,' said Pete, but he felt cold and stiff.

'We shan't be found out, don't you worry,' said Steve. 'Not so long as nobody grasses.'

'You don't need to keep on about it,' said Pete. 'D'you think I would?'

'Not unless you're a damn fool,' said Steve. 'Go on, if you're going. I want my tea, and we'd better not all be seen walking up together.'

'Right,' said Pete, and turned to go.

'Shall I go with him?' asked Vince.

'Yeah, may as well,' said Curly. 'He'd look funny, coming out from under the bridge on his own.'

Pete was glad Vince had suggested coming with him. They clambered back over the parapet, and walked slowly up the hill. No one was in sight, and as they passed the bus shelter, Pete drew Vince into it.

'Here,' he said, 'have these. I don't want them, truly, and they're yours by rights.' Vince looked pleased – he was a tubby boy, much given to sweet-eating – but he insisted that Pete should keep one bar of chocolate for himself.

'The others wouldn't like it if you had nothing,' he said. Both he and Pete realized why; if Pete knew what the others had been up to, then they would feel safer if he was as guilty as the rest of them; but neither said anything. Pete pocketed the bar of chocolate grudgingly and they went on up the street.

Sid's motorbike was still where he had left it. There was no sign of Sid, but while Vince was standing talking, they saw him coming along the road towards them, alone.

'I'd better get along then,' said Vince, and went.

Sid seemed quite pleased to see Pete, and apologized for keeping him waiting.

'It's all right,' said Pete. 'I saw some pals. 'Where've the others gone?' The others, it appeared, had settled down in the pub. The three boys had paid for a round of drinks, which had cleaned Sid out, and he left before the second round was due. Pete climbed on the bike, feeling secure and relieved tucked in close behind his cousin. They were different from these town boys with their uncomfortable freedom with money and possessions.

'All right?' called Sid, as the engine sputtered into life.

'Fine,' shouted Pete, and they roared away out of the town and into the quiet countryside.

Chapter 2

As they coasted down through the village towards Pete's home, he saw the cluster of cars parked outside the chapel and realized he was late. His mother always attended the fortnightly evening service. Sometimes Pete went with her, but on these long summer evenings he was often out, and she would not be worrying about him, probably guessing he was having tea with Tom up at Tygwyn. That meant the house would be empty, because Uncle Sam would be up at Grandpa's taking Aunt Emmy for her Sunday walk.

Aunt Emmy was something of an embarrassment to Pete. She was a sister of his mother's and of Uncle Sam, but she had never grown up: a stout middle-aged woman who saw herself a perpetual child in a world of adults. She used to treat Pete as a companion of her own age, and pick quarrels with him like a spoilt child, and he never knew what to do so he took to avoiding her whenever he could; but last time he saw her, after a gap of some months, she took his arm, admiringly, as though he were Uncle Sam, and asked him to take her for a walk. Pete had not been near the place since then, and yet he felt bad about it, because of his grandparents. His grandmother, crippled now with arthritis, was still able, painfully, to knit him the kind of sweaters he liked, and Grandpa, who carried trays and coals with slow patient hands, had taught Pete to whistle and to watch the weather and the birds.

Four times a week Pete's mother crossed the bridge and trudged up the road past the village school, a mile and a half to the roadside cottage where the grandparents lived with Aunt

Emmy. There she swept and cooked and passed on the news and praised Aunt Emmy for doing the washing-up nicely, or scolded her for not making her bed properly, and listened while Nana told her what the District Nurse had said, and Grandma compared the seasons with those of years long past. It was a way of life for her, and the reason why she did not go out to a job and earn a bit of extra money, as the wives of most men earning a labourer's wage did. Pete's father earned more on the road-building site than he could have done on a farm, but most of the extra was eaten away by the battered A.30 travelling to and fro across the country. Uncle Sam gave Pete a pound at Christmas and birthdays, but otherwise anything he had spare from a village policeman's pay went on clothes for Aunt Emmy and repairs to the cottage.

Pete's mother had not left any tea out for him, probably because she thought he would have it at Tygwyn, so he went and had a look round the larder. There was some cold potato in a bowl so he cut himself a thick round of bread, spread it liberally with butter, covered it with a layer of cold sliced potato and topped the lot with salad cream. One of the best things about looking after himself was that he could eat the kind of food he liked, instead of what his mother thought was the right kind of food for that time of day. He took it through into the living-room and switched on the television, but as he sat down in front of it he felt the hard outline of the bar of chocolate in his pocket. He took it out, looked at it with some distaste, and then walked over and put it in his satchel, hanging behind the door. He would eat the chocolate waiting for the school bus next morning, he decided.

When the television came on, it was a discussion programme, a lot of men in glasses getting hot and bothered about something of no interest to Pete, so he switched to the other side, where they were singing hymns in Welsh.

Pete switched the set off abruptly and stood gazing out of the window, disturbed by the afternoon's events. The evening sun was lying golden on the hills, and the crowded little room suddenly seemed a prison. School tomorrow, another whole wcck of it; then another dull weekend, then another week of school, and so on for years and years. He remembered he had a history test tomorrow, and fetching a text-book from his satchel, more for form's sake than anything else, he took it outside and went and lay down in the rough grass at the end of the garden, where the rhubarb grew in clumps beneath the straggly hedge that separated their plot from the Tygwyn fields.

Pete propped himself on his elbows and tried to concentrate on the page in front of him. Some of the longer grasses kept getting in his way, and he tore them up. A glossy black beetle scuttled off, and an urgent spider, her egg tucked between her legs. A few bluebells grew thinly in the hedgerow, and Pete heard a bumble-bee zooming uncertainly about, looking for the source of the honey smell. He could not locate it at first, and when he did he had to keep on watching until it landed on the bluebell. He got quite irritated with the bee, for taking such a long time about it, and when eventually it did hook its furry legs on to the bell, the whole stem sagged under its weight, until the flower nearly touched the ground. Pete put his finger against the stem and slid it gently upwards, straightening the flower, to see if the bee would stand its ground. It zizzed angrily, but kept on sucking. Pete turned back to his history, now and again glancing sideways to see how the bee was getting on, clambering methodically from bell to bell.

'Why, Pete,' called his mother, 'you here all on your own?' She came down the path towards him, taking off her chapel hat.

'I've got a bee,' said Pete, innocently.

'A what?' said his mother. 'Oh, you daft thing.' She bent down and parted the fat rhubarb leaves. 'That rhubarb's lasting on well this year,' she said. 'Glad to see you doing a spot of work, though I don't know why you have to leave it till Sunday.'

'Got a test tomorrow,' said Pete.

Mrs Jenkins turned her straw hat around in her hands, smoothing it into shape.

'We were talking about that school trip, after you'd gone,' she said. 'Sam and me. He'd like to help with a bit of it, he said, and we reckoned we could manage between us that way.'

Pete gently prodded the bee with a grass stem. It zizzed again, angrily, like a baby disturbed at its bottle, and went to the next bloom.

'Are you listening, Pete?'

'Yeah, I'm listening. I'm just thinking, that's all.'

'Now don't be silly, Pete. You know you'd love it when you got there, with all your friends, and I'd like you to go, really I would. You mightn't get another chance like it.'

'What about Dad?' said Pete.

'We'll have to ask him, of course, but he won't object, you know that.'

Pete knew that, but it made him resentful sometimes that all the family decisions were taken by his mum and Uncle Sam, not his father, just because he was always stuck in some caravan on a works site hundreds of miles away. Every week, regular as clockwork, Dad sent money home, unless it was one of the rare occasions when he came back for a few days himself, but he never said anything about how it should be spent. Pete had to admit that he had never heard his mother grumble that it was hard to make ends meet, or ask for more at difficult times of the year; the only time he had ever heard her mention money to his father was when she accused him of not keeping enough back for himself. 'You should look after yourself better,' she said to him severely.

'I do all right for myself,' he told her. 'There's not much to spend money *on* at these sites.'

'I'll bet a lot of them find something,' Mrs Jenkins commented. 'Horses and drink – and other things.'

'Oh, ah,' said Pete's dad, and there the matter dropped.

It would be nice to go on the school trip, Pete decided. Better than Aberafon on a Sunday afternoon. He frowned at the memory.

'I would like to go,' he said. 'If you're sure it's all right.' He would send his dad picture-postcards that he could pin on the wall of his caravan and show his mates. 'That's Cologne Cathedral; my boy's out there, on a school trip.'

'When do you have to let them know?' his mother asked.

'Yeah, there's that, too,' said Pete. 'I might not get in.'

'Oh, Pete, you should have told us earlier.'

'Don't worry, Mum, it'll probably be all right. The last date was meant to be last Friday, but Coot – the master, you know – said there were a few vacancies, and for us to ask at home and let him know on Monday. You have to pay a deposit – five pounds now, and then the rest later on.'

Mrs Jenkins relaxed. 'That's all right then. I can't let you have the five pounds tomorrow, because the post office won't be open before the bus goes, but you give your name in straightaway, and say you'll pay on Tuesday.'

Pete began to explain that Coot would not actually put your name on his list till you brought the deposit, but Mrs Jenkins did not seem bothered about that. 'Don't be silly, Pete,' she said. 'He must give us time to get the money out. No one carries five pounds around with them all the time.'

Pete did not say any more. Parents were like that about school. They could not be brought to understand that schoolteachers were not interested in reasons, only results.

So next day, when he got to school, he simply did not go and give in his name, but he watched the list on the noticeboard anxiously, and was relieved to see there were still two places at the end of the day. The next morning he presented his five pounds, and was told he could fill in his name on the list, last but one. He was quite surprised to realize how happy it made him to know that he really was one of the group, and he began to join eagerly in the conversation with the other boys who were going.

Each day that week at school, whenever Vince got Pete in a quiet corner, he would ask him if he was going to be able to get into town on Sunday. Each time, Pete said he didn't know, which was true enough, but Vince seemed awfully keen on having him. 'It's all very well for Curly,' he said. 'He's got Steve on the job with him. Being look-out all by yourself isn't much fun.'

In the end, by Thursday, Pete was saying yes, he'd try and get a lift with Sid. He did not feel at all happy about it, but there was precious little going on in Llanwern, and after all, on Monday, if he had not shown up, he could always say he had been unable to get a lift. So on Friday he actually brought the subject up himself.

'Where shall I meet you on Sunday, Vince?' he asked. Although Vince had talked about little else all week, he had not made any definite arrangement.

'Oh, yes,' said Vince, vaguely. 'I'd forgotten about that. Listen, Steve says better to leave it this week; if we go too often it will begin to look suspicious.' For a moment, Pete felt almost disappointed, but then a marvellous sense of freedom welled up in him. This, he knew, was going to be a happy weekend.

He laughed and teased like a mad thing on the bus going home, and made plans to spend the whole of Saturday going on an expedition with Tom.

It proved to be one of those outings when everything goes off even better than one hopes. The day dawned cloudy, but by the time he had met Tom and they had gathered up some of the young boys the sun began to come through. They bicycled up into the hills, the day growing hotter every moment, and spent timeless hours bathing in a mountain pool at the foot of a waterfall, and playing wild games upon the banks. When all the store of food had been eaten and their energies began at last to wilt, they slipped their clothes back over bathing-trunks dried in the sun, and coasted silently homeward.

'We'll be getting the sheep down for shearing tomorrow,' said Tom. 'Coming?' So on Sunday, as soon as dinner was over, Pete went up in the Tygwyn Land-rover, and helped bring the crying flock down the road to the farm. Their soft hooves pattered, pattered, on the tarmac, and the warm smells of hot wool and sheep-droppings drifted with them like a cloud. The boys ran ahead to cut off likely false turns, or doubled back up to hurry the dawdlers, whooping and smacking their sticks on the ground. At the end of it lay a great tea in the old kitchen in Tygwyn, where Pete ate till he could eat no more, and washed it down with as much cider as he could decently persuade Mr Thomas to give him, after which the boys vied with Tom's two elder sisters at telling funny and irreverent jokes about the teachers at school.

When he got home, his mother was just addressing an envelope to his father. She looked up as Pete came in, and said, 'I've just written to let him know about the school trip. I expect he'll be pleased.'

'He'd better be,' said Pete cheerfully. Mrs Jenkins went to get a stamp, and Pete studied the address written, rather high up on the envelope, in his mother's careful hand.

'Mr Jenkins, c/o A.R.C.S. Construction Company Ltd, Site Office, Bentyre, Isle of Kell, Scotland,' he read.

'I didn't know Dad was working on an island,' he said aloud when his mother came back.

'Didn't you?' she said. 'He's been there some weeks now. Ever since he went back last time.'

'I knew it was Scotland, but I didn't know it was an island. How does he get his car there?'

'I don't know, love. Perhaps he leaves it on the mainland.

You'll have to ask him.' It was the kind of problem that did not interest Mrs Jenkins. 'It's a lonely place, by his account,' she went on. 'All mountains and sea, and scarcely a house to be seen. I think he said this was the first proper main road on the island.'

'Is it on the west coast?'

'I don't rightly know, love. It's a terrible long way, that's all I know. He said it weren't no use coming home until he had at least a week to put together.'

'There's an awful lot of islands on the west coast.'

'Is that so? D'you learn that in school? It's one of the Hebrides, I think he said.'

'That's on the west coast,' said Pete. 'I wonder if Kell is marked in my school atlas?' He went and fetched his atlas from his satchel, and found the map of Scotland. 'There are the Hebrides, I think.' He peered closely at the text. 'O-U-TE – Yeah, Outer Hebrides, that's right. And where's Skye? That's the Inner Hebrides. Which lot is Kell in?'

'I don't know, I'm sure. Let's have a look, Pete.' He showed her the atlas. 'What, all those little things there? You'll have to read the names to me, Pete. I can't see them without my glasses.'

'There's Lewis, and North something I can't pronounce; that big one's Mull . . .'

'He said something about Mull . . .'

'Hey, and here's Kell; it's quite big, really.'

'What, that little dot? It don't look big to me.'

'That's because the scale is small. You can see the scale by the edge somewhere. Yeah, here it is. It's thirty-two miles, just that little bit.'

'I can't see that without my glasses.'

'I'll get them for you.'

'Don't trouble.' Mrs Jenkins smiled. 'I didn't know you were so keen on maps and that. They must teach you *something* in school.'

Pete was staring at the small green blot, just separated by a sliver of blue from the knobbly outline of the mainland. All mountains and sea. A jumble of caravans and tin huts and one road on the island. Hardly a house to be seen. You could only get there by boat. The mountains reached to a little point marked in as dark a shade of brown as those near his home, but here he was miles from the sea. There the sea was all around that little brown speck on Kell. Did the mountains rise up in great cliffs from the water's edge, Pete wondered? The only seaside he had ever seen was the busy peopled resorts at Barry Island and Porthcawl, where he had been on Sunday School outings, and the long flat expanse of sand backing on to the marshes at Borth. None of those seemed to fit into the picture of Kell.

'Mum,' he said.

'I'm in the kitchen,' Mrs Jenkins called. She must have gone while he was staring at the map. He went through and found her wiping the dishes.

'Mum,' he said again, 'why can't I go and stay with Dad in his caravan sometimes during the holidays?'

She was silent so long he thought she could not have heard him.

'Mum,' he said at last. 'Did you hear what I said?'

She turned then, slowly polishing a plate. 'Yes,' she said, 'I heard you. I was thinking, that's all.' Pete waited. It was no use trying to hurry his mother when she was thinking.

'There's no reason why not,' she said at length, 'when you're a bit older. If your dad agrees, that is.'

'I'm thirteen.'

'I know, Pete. But it's a long way, and would cost a lot of money, and what would you do with yourself all day?'

'I'd find something.'

'Well, you can't go this summer, any road, because of the school trip, and not at Christmas, because of the weather, and anyway there wouldn't be time. We'll think about it next summer.'

'But that's a long time away. Why can't I go back with him after his next lot of days off? I'll be back from Germany by then, and the autumn term won't have started.'

'And where's all that money coming from? You'd still have the train fare coming back, and no one to make the journey with you. Why all this sudden rush, anyway?'

'Dad probably will have finished up there by then – the island isn't *that* big – and be working somewhere dreary like the outskirts of Birmingham, and I know you wouldn't let me go to that sort of place.'

'Like as not,' agreed Mrs Jenkins placidly. 'I don't know what makes you so keen on the idea anyway. You've got a comfortable home here, and you can't say I don't let you have freedom to do what you want. It wouldn't be like a holiday camp, living out on one of them sites, whatever you may think.'

Pete turned away, abruptly. 'It would be a nice change,' he said, 'to see my own father sometimes.'

'You know he comes home as often as he can, and anyway you've got Grandad and Uncle Sam, who's as good to you as any father,' Mrs Jenkins began. Then she broke off. When she spoke again, there was a dawning surprise in her voice. 'I didn't know you felt that way,' she said.

Pete did not answer. He had not realized he felt that way himself until the words were out.

'I must finish my history,' he said, without turning round.

'Perhaps one day he can get a job nearer home,' said his mother. 'Then he could be home a lot more often. But you know how it is round here, for jobs.'

'I've got my homework to do,' Pete said shortly, and left the room.

Chapter 3

LATER that week, Mrs Jenkins gave Pete ten pounds to take to school towards the expenses of the trip. Otherwise life went on uneventfully, and to Pete's relief neither Vince nor the other two boys brought up the subject of the tobacconist again. The following week, his mother gave him another ten pounds.

'That's from Uncle Sam,' she said. 'I'll let you have the remaining ten next week.'

The school trip was due to start a week before the end of term. As the time drew nearer, interest mounted among the group who were going; those who were not, grumbled freely about the extra five days' holiday they were missing, and those who were, kept on being called to meetings where Coot announced further details about the arrangements and gave them sheafs of notices and forms to take home, so that even at home there seemed to be only one thing to talk about. In the mounting excitement, Pete quite forgot how off-hand and unenthusiastic he had been about the venture at the beginning.

In school, Pete was seeing more of Tom, and less of Vince. There wasn't anything to talk to Vince *about*, because Vince wasn't interested in the school trip, and Pete did not want to mention the tobacconist. They did, however, sit next to each other, so they had to find something to talk about.

'I shall be glad when the football season starts again,' said Pete one dull wet afternoon. Someone had brought his transistor to school, and a group of boys were huddled around the muttering box listening to a commentary on a county cricket match. Pete and Vince were not near enough to hear what was going on, and were not specially interested.

'It'll be starting next month, I should think,' said Vince. 'Anyway, Cardiff have got a match at the end of next week against some European team. They've got to fit it in before the real stuff starts. You'll be away, though.'

'I shouldn't have been able to go anyway, I don't suppose,' observed Pete. 'Who are they playing?'

'I forget where they come from. Might be Rumania, or Hungary or somewhere like that. Curly told me. They're called the Zodiaks.'

'Is he going?'

'And me too, if we can get the money.'

'Some people have all the luck.'

'Hey, who's talking? If you weren't going on the trip, just think how many home matches you could get to next season.'

Pete turned moodily to his desk as the bell rang. 'Try telling that to my mum,' he said. 'She doesn't think football matches are educational.'

'You want to get a job in the holidays, then it's your own money,' said Vince. 'That's what Curly and I are going to do.'

'How are you going to get it for the Zodiak match?' asked Pete.

'That's the trouble. But Curly said not to worry – he'll think of something,' said Vince.

Pete wondered how Curly was going to think himself three pounds, which is what it would cost to get two boys to Cardiff and back and into the football ground, but the teacher came in at that moment for the first lesson of the afternoon, so he dropped the subject.

Then on Friday, three things happened.

In the dinner-hour, Pete got a note asking him to go and see Mr Turner at the staff-room door. Mr Turner was Coot, so called because he had lank black hair falling down on each side of the bald patch where his hair-line had receded. He had a sloping forehead that continued into his nose in a straight line, and a way of bobbing his head backwards and forwards when he walked. He looked, in fact, just like a coot.

Pete knocked at the staff-room door, and Coot himself opened it.

'Did you want me, sir?' asked Pete. He had not been searching his conscience because Coot wasn't one of those who made an issue out of little things.

'Oh, yes, Jenkins.' Coot shut the door behind him, and bobbed his head anxiously. 'I'm afraid I've got some bad news for you. That is, if you've been looking forward very much to this trip.'

Pete stared at him blankly. 'Why, sir?'

'Well, it seems the travel agents have made a bit of a mix-up and they've booked us two places short. I phoned them as soon as I discovered it, but it seems there's nothing they can do about it. I've discussed the matter with the Head, and we decided the only thing to do was to leave out the two last to book – which happens to be you and Sally Price.'

'You mean, I can't go?'

'I'm awfully sorry, Jenkins, but it did seem the fairest way. Of course, if anyone drops out, you'd have their place.' He brightened. 'It's quite possible, you know. Last year we had two or three last-minute drop-outs.'

'What about Sally Price?'

'Well, her name was last on the list, after yours, so if a vacancy does occur, you'd get the first chance of it.'

'Thank you very much,' said Pete. There did not seem anything else to say.

'I'm terribly sorry about this.' Coot's head still bobbed anxiously up and down. 'As you know, I've been running these visits for years, and this is the first time this has happened. I hope you're not too disappointed?'

He sounded so forlorn that Pete felt he must cheer him up.

'It's all right, sir,' he said. 'I don't mind.' But he did.

'There really is a chance a place might crop up,' Coot assured him earnestly.

Pete was surprised at himself for being so disappointed, and on top of that was the uncomfortable thought that he would have to tell his mother he could not go after all. When he got back to the class-room, Tom and some of the others were talking to the form who had been last year about the channel crossing.

'And there was Foxy sitting down in front of this plateful of chips and sausages and fried eggs, and everyone was giving him their helpings, because the boat was going uhh-ahh – (hands expressively see-sawing) – and everyone else was going greener and greener, and suddenly poor old Gegs here went belting up on deck, and ...'

Everybody was laughing so Pete joined in. He couldn't get hold of the idea that he did not belong to this group any more, that they were all talking about adventures they could look forward to sharing together, all except for him. He decided not to say anything about his conversation with Coot, not just yet, anyway. Someone might drop out, as Coot had said, and he could go after all. Even if they didn't, he could go on pretending a little bit longer. All the same, the sad truth kept nagging at him through afternoon school and by the time the bell rang for the end of the last lesson he was feeling pretty fed up.

Then, while he was getting his things from the cloakroom, Vince came up to him.

'It's this Sunday,' he said. 'It's on. Curly said be sure to come, because it's important.'

'What's on?' said Pete, but he knew.

'Shh! You know. Bongo's.'

'Oh,' said Pete. 'What if I can't get a lift?'

'You've got to, somehow. Curly and Steve say it's really important to have two look-outs, and I want you, anyway. It'll be the last time, I expect.'

'Why's that?'

'Steve says you should never go on raiding the same place. People get suspicious. Even Bongo, he reckons.'

The last time. That was something, and it would be a bit of excitement. The weekend was going to be pretty dreary now there was no school trip to make plans for. His mum would be grumbling, saying he should have let her know about it sooner, and then he would not have been one of the last on the list.

'O.K.,' he said. 'I'll try. But I can't promise. I don't want Mum and Uncle Sam to get to know; after all, it would look strange, wouldn't it? They think I always stick around the village on a Sunday.'

'You scared?'

'No, of course not. It's just sense. I'll come if I can, I promise.'

'It shouldn't be difficult. Sid has been in every Sunday since he had his bike. I know 'cos I've seen him. All you've got to do is be out on the road somewhere out of sight of the village, and he'll pick you up.'

Pete did not know Sid's visits were that regular. He'd been with Tom on recent Sundays, and had not given much thought to Sid and his bike. He turned, and saw that Vince was watching him.

'I'll be there,' he said, walking towards the passage. Tom was strolling down the corridor towards him, and stopped when he saw him approaching.

'Come *on*,' said Tom. 'The girls will have pinched the back seat in the bus. Whatever's keeping you?'

'Hey, Pete,' Vince called after him in an urgent whisper.

'What is it?' asked Pete. 'Hang on a minute,' he shouted to Tom. Then he turned back to Vince. 'What is it?'

'The meeting-place – not by Bongo's, that's too dangerous. Under the bridge where we went last time, at half past three.'

'All right,' said Pete.

'Sure, now? You won't be late?'

'All *right*,' said Pete. He turned to go, and Tom was standing in the doorway immediately behind him. 'Coming,' he said.

Vince pulled his sleeve as he was going. 'Hi, Pete.'

'Yeah?'

Vince looked pointedly at Tom's back view, and put his finger to his lips.

'All *right*,' said Pete crossly.

'What's the matter with Vince?' asked Tom as they crossed the yard.

'Oh, nothing. He was just being stupid, that's all.'

'I always said he was a daft nit,' remarked Tom, climbing on to the bus. He gave a groan. 'Told you so. Let's sit here.' The back seat was already full of girls, gabbling like hens. 'Hey, did I tell you about Alan coming?'

'No.'

'He's coming to stay with us after we get back from Germany. That'll be great. We'll have some fun, you'll see.'

'Great,' Pete agreed politely. He did not feel very enthusiastic. He and Tom could have plenty of fun together without an unknown cousin having to be around.

On Fridays Mrs Jenkins stayed late up at the grandparents, as she would not be up there again until Monday. Pete used to stay on the school bus and drop off at the cottage and have tea with Nana and Grandad and Aunt Emmy and come home with his mum, but lately, in order to avoid Aunt Emmy, he had been making an excuse of his homework and having tea with Tom at Tygwyn, saying they could do their work together after tea. They could, but usually they didn't.

That day, as usual, they took their tea, on plates, from the kitchen table where it was all laid out, and went through into the living-room to watch television. Gary, Tom's younger brother, was with them. There was an adventure serial on, which they had been following for a couple of weeks, about a gang of boys and girls who tracked down and unmasked some burglars.

'They took an awful long time to spot who done it,' said Gary. 'I could tell ages ago.'

'I bet you wouldn't, though, in real life,' said Pete. 'In a story, you know something like that is going to happen, but in ordinary living you don't. You just kind of expect everyone to be normal.'

'Trouble is, everything *is* normal somewhere like this,' said Gary. 'Nobody ever robs Mrs Burns's shop or anything exciting like that.'

'Hey, but it does happen!' cried Tom suddenly. Tom had a most expressive face, and when something caught his imagination his eyes were like stars and his very freckles seemed to dance with life. 'You know, Pete, Bongo's!'

'Bongo's?' said Pete. His skin prickled. There was nothing else he could say.

'Whoever's Bongo?' asked Gary. 'Bongo, Bongo.' He giggled. 'Sounds like a cartoon.' Gary still attended the village primary school.

'He's a funny old man who keeps a sweet shop near the school,' said Tom. 'Most of us get our sweets there, because he has lots of gum and sherbets and that sort of stuff, and he doesn't mind how long we take to choose. Everything's always in an awful muddle and I shouldn't think he ever *dusts* anything, would you, Pete?'

'I doubt it,' said Pete, with an effort.

'What about Bongo, anyway?' said Gary. 'Bongo, Bongo,' he repeated to himself with relish.

'He's been broken into, and had things pinched,' said Tom. 'More than once, in the last few weeks, so it's probably someone local. That's what the police think.'

'The police?' said Pete. 'Do they know about it?'

'Of course,' said Tom. 'Naturally Bongo reported it, and they were in his shop making inquiries when some of the boys were there after school yesterday.' He paused and looked at Pete's blank face. 'Weren't you there when we were talking about it after dinner today?'

'I had to go and see Coot about something,' said Pete mechanically.

'Oh, yeah, that's right. Do you mean to say you didn't know about it?'

'No,' said Pete. He felt all shrivelled up inside. 'Not a thing. Tell me.'

'Well, apparently he first noticed a few things were missing some weeks back – nothing much, some sweets and maybe one or two packets of cigarettes. He thought someone must be pinching them behind his back in the shop, while he was serving, but he wasn't sure. Being Bongo, I wonder he noticed at all. So then he marked a few things underneath, thinking he wouldn't sell them, and if they disappeared, then he'd know they'd been pinched.

'How did he mark them?'

'Oh, I don't know – put a cross on the wrapper, I suppose, something like that. Anyway, they disappeared and the old boy just puzzled about it for a long time, because he'd been keeping an eye on the marked stuff, and he never saw anybody take it, and at last it sank in that maybe it wasn't just somebody grabbing a bit extra while they was in the shop, but someone breaking in when the shop was closed, like over the weekend.'

'I don't see what difference that makes,' said Gary.

'Yeah, it was still only a few sweets,' said Pete.

'Ah,' said Tom, 'that's just it. It wasn't.'

'Wasn't?' said Pete.

'No. Of course, even old Bongo doesn't leave a till full of money in his shop all weekend – he probably needs the cash, anyway, but you know that money-box thing he's got, shaped like a house, for money for Children's Homes or something – you put the money through a slot in the roof?'

'Yeah, I know; does anyone ever put anything in?'

'Well, they must, because every so often, whenever Bongo thinks it's getting a bit full, or he wants some change, he takes out ten bob's worth of coins, or maybe a quid, and puts it in the till, and puts a fifty-pence piece or a pound note in an old tobacco tin on the back shelf, where I suppose he thought it was safe enough, and no one would ever think of looking.'

'And had it gone?' asked Gary, eagerly.

'I suppose some bloke comes once a year or so to collect the money, but he hadn't been lately, and there were four pound notes there, according to Bongo. And then he goes to put in another quid a couple of days ago, and the tin was empty!'

'He must have made a mistake,' said Pete.

'Why should he? It isn't as though he's got to account for that money – I mean no one but him knows how much he's collected, so he hasn't got to say anything about it. He wouldn't, unless he was sure.'

'Four pounds!' Pete could not believe it. 'Four pounds!' he said again.

'It's not that much,' said Gary. The other boys looked surprised, and Gary hastened to explain. 'I don't mean it doesn't matter; but you were saying, Tom, as we could be like the children in the serial, and set out to catch a gang of robbers. But those men on the T.V., they were real thieves, they were after thousands of pounds.'

'But don't you see, that makes it all the more difficult!' Tom was vibrant with eagerness again. 'It calls for real detective work. If it was a gang of professional thieves, the police would soon pick them out in a little place like Aberafon . . .'

'How?'

'Because either they'd be strangers, or if they lived there they'd be spending lots of money that nobody had seen them earning. But to watch out for four pounds being spent that you have reason to believe has been stolen . . . It's a pity,' he went on thoughtfully, 'that old Bongo didn't think to mark those pound notes.'

'Perhaps he did,' said Gary hopefully.

Tom shook his head. 'No,' he said, 'he wouldn't have done that, because he didn't think of them getting stolen. I know! I'll tell you what he ought to do. He ought to mark some more notes, and put them in there . . . We could tell him, Pete! We'll go and see him on Monday, and tell him our plan, and say he's to put those notes marked with a special sign, in his tin, and leave them there, just as before; and then we can slip around the shops and ask them to keep a look-out in case anyone tries to pass off the marked notes.'

'And the banks – don't people pay money into banks?' asked Gary.

'Yeah,' said Tom, more doubtfully. The thought of two thirteen-year-old boys telling bank managers to look out for marked money in those grand establishments which Tom had never entered in his life, brought him down to earth. 'Maybe the police had better arrange with the banks and the post office and those kind of places,' he said. 'I wish Alan were here now. He'd know what to do, I bet.'

'Maybe the police would rather do it all themselves,' Pete managed to say sarcastically, but a fearful thought struck him. Supposing they were, even now, doing just that? How could he warn Curly and Steve and Vince? Hard on the heels of that thought came another, angry one. Why should he warn them, anyway? They had lied to him about the money – Vince had said they weren't taking any money. No, perhaps Vince wasn't lying; he had been look-out, and had not seen what the other two were up to any more than Pete. He remembered Curly looking meaningfully at Steve when Vince had said that about them not stealing money, and Steve had just looked blank and indifferent. And he thought how he, Pete, had knowingly taken and eaten a stolen Crunchie – marked, perhaps, too – and a bar of chocolate, and accepted a stolen fag, and chucked it in the river.

He looked across at Tom, all glowing and eager to act the detective, inviting him to hunt down the thieves and protect poor old Bongo.

'How do you think we should go about it, Pete?' Tom asked. 'Do you think it's leaving it too late to wait until Monday before we see Bongo?'

'No,' said Pete. 'I should think Monday will be time enough.' He hoped Tom would not ask him why he thought that.

'Can't I help?' asked Gary.

'I don't see how you can,' said Tom. 'You're never in town.'

'I wish I could,' said Gary. 'I'll think up bright ideas.'

'You do that,' said Tom. 'We could do with some. Haven't you any suspicions, Pete, as to who it could be?'

'No,' said Pete, quickly. 'Have you?'

'I'm just thinking. If it were what Bongo thought at first, someone nicking a few sweets while they were in the shop, I'd think it might be someone from school. But this is real stealing – breaking into the shop and taking money – that wouldn't be anyone from our school.' He thought a moment. 'Probably someone quite young, though, taking those sweets, unless they've got kids.' He paused, slightly embarrassed. 'Pete,' he said at last, 'you don't think it could be those boys Sid goes around with, do you?'

'Why them?' snapped Pete.

'Only that they're often around town on a Sunday, and – well, Sid's got a new bike, and the others go to the pub quite a bit, I've heard.'

'They've all got jobs. They don't need to nick four quid to have a drink. Anyway, why pick on Sid?'

'All right, all right. I know he's your cousin, but there's no need to get so windy about it.'

No indeed. Pete could imagine what his mum would have to say if Sid were known to be stealing from shops. How would she feel if the real truth came out? Again that cold shrivelled feeling clenched him inside.

'I must go, Tom. I'll try and think who it could be.'

Tom looked at him in surprise. 'What have you got to go for? We haven't any homework worth speaking of, now there's only a week to the end of term.'

'Fortnight,' said Pete. He walked out into the yard. Tom came with him.

'Yeah, officially, I know, but only a week for us, because of the trip. You know, Pete, it's great you were able to come after all. I'm awfully looking forward to it, aren't you?'

Pete grunted, and looked away.

'That reminds me,' Tom went on cheerfully. 'What did old Coot want you for?'

There was a pause. 'Oh, *that*,' said Pete slowly, to fill the gap. What should he say? The pause seemed endless. Quick, he must say *something*. He looked at Tom, so eager and friendly, and then glanced round to see if Gary had followed them. He hadn't. They were alone in the yard.

Pete drew a deep breath to steady his voice. 'I might not be coming on the trip,' he said evenly.

Tom exclaimed, 'Oh, Pete, why ever not?'

It was a relief to tell someone. They walked across the yard and leant against the low stone wall by the lane, and Pete explained what had happened.

'That's not fair!' Tom grumbled, and added, 'I bet your mum will be cross about it.'

'Yeah,' said Pete gloomily. 'I hope she doesn't try and make a fuss at school about it. There's no point making a fuss.' Fussing parents just made you look a fool; they never did any good. Then he brightened. 'There's still a chance I might be able to go. Coot said I could have first place if anyone dropped out.'

'I remember last year quite a few couldn't go at the last minute and they had a job making up the numbers,' said Tom.

'Oh, don't worry, Pete. You'll be able to go, I'm sure of it.'

'Listen,' said Pete. 'Don't say anything to my mum, or to your people, about it, not just yet. I don't want her fussing for nothing.'

'You'll have to tell her some time,' said Tom.

'Not if an extra place turns up,' said Pete. 'And if it doesn't, I don't want her going on about it all this weekend, do I?'

Tom agreed. As they leant together on the sun-warmed wall, picking little bits of dried moss out of the cracks and flicking them at each other, they heard the tractor coming down the lane, with the creaking noise of an implement dragging along the tarmac behind it.

'That's the turner,' said Tom. 'I wonder whose field that is?'

At that moment the tractor came into view, with Tom's brother Kevin at the wheel, and the tines of the turner vibrating as the iron-rimmed wheels jolted along the lane.

'Where've you been?' yelled Tom above the tractor's roar.

'Up at the Rhos,' shouted Kevin. 'Be hauling up there tomorrow.' The boys turned and followed him through the yard, and came and stood by him as he unhitched the turner. 'If this weather holds,' Kevin went on, 'Eddy will run the pheasant over the top field tomorrow – the one I've just been turning now – in the morning, and we'll be able to bale it in the afternoon, and with any luck get the lot hauled before dark.' The turner simply runs down the lines of mown hay turning the dank green side uppermost to face the sun, but the pheasant froths and tosses it so that the air can get right into the heart of the swathes.

'Where's Dad?' asked Tom.

'Baling at Pugh's,' said Kevin. The baler was too expensive a piece of machinery for every farmer to own. The Thomases had one, and all the farmers around borrowed it, occasionally for payment, but most of the neighbours simply earned their share of it by helping Thomas with his harvest. In fact, everyone worked as a team on each farm in turn, but as Thomas had the highest acreage, involving the most labour, it was tacitly assumed that he would loan out the more expensive items of machinery.

'I thought I heard the mower in the Bottom Meadow,' said Pete. That was the field that ran down from the farm to the river, behind Pete's house, and where he had watched the lark descending into the lush grass nearly three weeks ago.

'Oh, that must be Eddy,' said Kevin. Eddy Price was the farmer up at the Rhos, where Kevin had been turning. 'He was cutting his own second field when I went up there, and he said he'd come on down to us as soon as he'd finished.' The three of them, joined by Gary, strolled across the yard to where they could look over on to the Bottom Meadow. It was a big field, gently sloping down to the line of alders that marked the stream at the far side. Over the hedge to the right Pete could see the red roofs of the village, his own house among them. The sight of it reminded him of problems he would rather forget.

The outer rim of the field had been mown for a width of some twenty yards a couple of days before, and the hay already looked bleached and dry against the light green of the shaved grass between the swathes. The next twenty yards or so, geometrically enclosed in a rectangle within the outer border, was also cut, but here the lines of fallen grass were a rich green, and the gold of the buttercups and the white of the moondaisies could still be distinguished together with the silvery-grey of the thistles, but were fast fading in the July heat. Within this again stood the last block of uncut grass, casting a long shadow at the eastern edge, because the sun was getting low. Here the swathes fell steadily and neatly as the tractor snarled its way along the edge and the blades of the mower slid along the roots behind and to the side of the tractor.

'Looks as though that first lot will be ready for hauling by Sunday,' observed Kevin. 'That is, if the weather holds.'

'What about the football field?' asked Tom. 'I see that's baled as we came past in the bus.'

'I think we might get that in tonight,' said Kevin. 'Only I wish Dad would come back soon; I don't want to start on it until he's seen it.'

'Oh, great!' exclaimed Gary. 'We can start playing football again.' The football field was so called because it was where the village boys always played their games. It lay behind the farm, bordering the main road, and was flatter than anywhere else.

Kevin laughed. 'There won't be much football for anyone this weekend,' he said. 'Not if the weather holds.' He looked at his watch. 'I think I'll take the van and see if I can find Dad, so's we can get going on that field. You can go up there and start rolling bales if you like.'

'What if we don't like?' said Gary, but Kevin merely punched him playfully, and went to get the van out.

As the boys walked slowly to the football field, Pete began to feel a lot happier. Tom had been comforting about the school trip, and as for the other thing – Bongo's – well, it looked as though he could forget about it for two days. When hay-making started in earnest, nobody old enough to steer a tractor or shift a bale was too young to help, and there was no question of Tom slipping into Aberafon to rush to Bongo's aid. And it was a grand excuse for Pete. He did not *have* to help with the hay harvest, but it was assumed he would, and if he was not with the other boys on Sunday then questions would be asked.

In any case, if Tom had heard the boys at school discussing the burglary at Bongo's, the chances were that Vince had too, or Curly and Steve, in which case they would certainly call off Sunday's escapade, and would not be at all pleased if Pete called attention to them by turning up in town to look for them. The trouble was that all those three went home for dinner, so could easily have missed the gossip, as Pete had.

This was an uncomfortable thought, and Pete quelled it hastily. Surely some of the rumours would have spilled over into the last few minutes of the dinner-break and been taken up afresh by the home dinner boys as they returned? Not in Pete's form, he knew, or Vince would have sought him out about it, but even if Vince had missed hearing anything, there was a good chance that Curly or Steve had stumbled on the story.

Anyway, he was fed up with worrying. The best thing he could do was to throw himself into hay-making and forget all his troubles until Monday.

Chapter 4

BY the time Pete went to bed on Sunday night, his skin was burning from the days spent shirtless in the sunny fields, and smarting from the thousands of tiny scratches and pricks gained from lugging the heavy bales about, the dried grass-heads and, worse, the thistles, scraping on bare arms and chest. The brightness of the fields and the musty gloom of the barn alternated behind his closed eyelids, and the sheets felt cool and comforting. The labours of the weekend concertina-ed in his sleepy brain, always the same, yet marked off in little differences – the same sun, the same scratchy bales, heaved across the field, heaved on to the trailer, heaved off the trailer, heaved into the barn, heaved into place in the stack, but the sun in different quarters of the cloudless sky, different fields, different barns, different farmers taking the decisions, different farmer's wives giving ample teas in different farm kitchens.

Oh, the joy of being utterly exhausted and comfortable in bed at the end of the day! What about Bongo, and Vince, and Curly and Steve? Don't worry, Pete told himself. No doubt they would have heard the rumours, and called the whole thing off, thankful, probably, that Pete had not complicated things by turning up in the middle of Sunday afternoon. Anyhow, it was all much too far away and unimportant to worry about. The only thing that mattered was sleep.

The next morning he got up and caught the bus in the same contented frame of mind. Somebody would have dropped out of the school trip, Curly and the others would have steered clear of the tobacconist's, the police would not have discovered anything. As the bus pulled up the hill out of the village, he and Tom could see over the hedges into the neat empty grasslands where they had toiled for the past two days. After so much hard work it was only fair that everything should turn out right for him.

The mood lasted till he was in school. The bus was rather late getting in that morning, so they did not go to their classrooms, but unshouldered their satchels on the lockers in the cloakroom and went straight into assembly. Coot was hanging about in the passage, having a word with each member of the Germany group as they passed.

'You still all right for Friday?' he said to Tom.

'Yes, sir,' said Tom. 'Why?'

'Just checking numbers,' murmured Coot. Then he drew Pete aside. 'Richard Davies has had to drop out,' he said, 'so that means you can have his place – if you still want it, that is.'

'Yes, please, sir,' said Pete. 'Thank you very much.' He felt he must add, 'What about Sally Price? She was on the list, too,' but he got the answer he hoped for.

'First come, first served,' said Coot. 'That's only fair. Maybe another vacancy will occur, but anyhow this place is yours.'

'Oh, thank you, sir,' said Pete. 'That's great.' And he marched gaily into the gym. Tom had gone ahead, so Pete found himself at the end of a row next to a couple of girls.

The Head was looking more than usually harassed, and at the end of morning assembly he did an odd thing. He dismissed the girls and told the boys to stay behind.

'Hey, what have you been up to?' muttered the girl next to Pete, as she turned to go. She meant the boys generally, but it gave Pete a spasm of conscience.

'Probably a holiday, for good work – boys only,' he managed to say.

'Get away!' she said, and was gone. Pete was left standing on his own, separated by a great gap from the next boy. He wanted to shuffle along and merge into the flock, but was afraid to draw attention to himself.

Then, suddenly, through the thinning ranks, he saw old Bongo standing beside the deputy headmistress, by the main entrance. His heart froze.

The headmaster waited carefully until the doors had closed behind the last girl, and then told them, with great gravity, about the pilfering from the tobacconist's. 'Yesterday,' he went on, 'Mr Williamson was actually sitting quietly in his shop when the culprits broke in. When they saw him they turned and ran away, but he had time to see them perfectly well, and I am very sorry to have to say that he recognized them as boys from this school whom he has frequently served when they come into his shop on weekdays wearing school uniform.' He paused and an expectant stillness filled the room. Only the eyes of the boys moved, scanning the ranks in front for a guilty move, or a likely offender. The boys in the front row grew pink with the effort of trying to see out of the backs of their heads.

'I would ask,' the headmaster went on in measured terms, 'I would ask the boys who must know they are responsible to step forward.' Again the expectant stillness. Some daring wag behind Pete muttered, 'He'll be lucky.' 'If they do not,' continued the Head, 'then I shall require all the boys to go out through the main entrance in single file on their way to their lessons, and Mr Williamson will then, no doubt, be able to pick out the two boys whom he saw. Before I tell the front row to lead off, I will give the culprits another chance to come forward of their own free will.'

Pete swivelled his eyes around as far as they would go, looking for Vince. He could not see him, but he suddenly saw Curly and Steve standing together not far away from him. Curly was unnaturally rigid, and sweating slightly. Pete could only see the back of Steve's head, but he looked lounging, relaxed, and unconcerned.

The little boy at the end of the front row had his eyes fixed anxiously on the Head's face, and when the Head gave a brisk nod to him he bolted out like a frightened rabbit, the rest of the line following him. The Head did not seem too bothered about this helter-skelter flight while it concerned the first form, but then he slowed it down. Pete, because he was late, was out of form order, so he was able to see Vince as he approached the exit. Old Bongo made a move as though to check him, and then let him go. He was very like Curly, and Bongo's reaction was not lost on Curly, not far behind in the line. He whispered something in Steve's ear, tugging at his sleeve – perhaps suggesting they should own up? Pete could not tell – but Steve affected not to notice. He was watching Bongo with an air of condescending amusement, peering anxiously up from hunched shoulders at each boy's face in turn. Bongo must have felt his eyes upon him, because he was suddenly watching him as he approached along the line, and after that he did not bother to look at the nearer boys as they passed.

As soon as Steve and Curly got to him, the old man pointed them out to the Head, who called them to stand on one side. The lines moved faster after that, as though everybody knew the business was done. As Pete went by his cheeks were red, and he took care not to look at the two older boys. Then, to his horror, Steve spoke.

'Hullo, Pete,' he said casually. 'We missed you yesterday. We thought you must be ill.'

Pete swung round and in a single startled moment he saw the rows of faces turn to him – Steve, angry and contemptuous. Curly, plainly unhappy, Bongo, suddenly alert, the Head, glancing from Steve to Pete with cool appraisal, and then, beyond him, at the end of the next row back, Tom – Tom with a look of pure astonishment which turned, as his eye met Pete's, to a sort of distant hostility. He had not known Tom was just behind him.

In the corridor, Pete waited where he could see Tom approaching, trying to catch his eye so that he could smile at him and force him to smile back, but when Tom did look at him again it was with a blank unsmiling iron face, that passed from Pete's eyes down over his blazer and on to the wall beside him without a glimmer of expression. Pete turned away and went to his class-room, alone.

Vince was already there, at his desk. He looked Pete over with as little friendliness as Tom, but he had to speak to him. 'I suppose they got them?' was all he said. Pete nodded.

'What happened – yesterday?' he said at last.

'Well, *you* should know,' said Vince.

'Why me? I wasn't there.'

'No. Why not? Because you knew what was going to happen, see.'

'Vince! I didn't! Honest I didn't! I couldn't come because I was . . .' he suddenly saw Tom's cool eye upon him; 'I was hay-making,' he finished lamely.

'What did happen, Vince?' another boy asked. The whole class was silently attentive.

'Curly and Steve pushed open the door of the shop – they could see it wasn't locked properly, see? – just to pick up a few sweets, that's all – and old Bongo was sitting there behind his counter, sort of hidden behind the newspaper stand. It was only when they went round behind the counter they seen him.'

'Was it them that had been going before?'

Vince looked cornered. 'I don't know. Shouldn't think so. Could have been.'

'Probably,' said the tormentor, coolly. 'Because whoever it was had been taking the homeless children's money from a tin round behind the counter. I expect that's what they were after this time, too. If it had just been snatching a few sweets and scarpering they might have got away with it.'

'You don't know nothing about it,' said Vince angrily.

'And what,' said somebody else – it wasn't Tom, he was silent – 'what had Pete got to do with it?'

Piece by piece, the mean little story came out. By dinner-time, Steve's and Curly's parents had been seen going to the headmaster's room, and so had a policeman. Later Vince was summoned; he returned limp but relieved. He was not going to be charged with anything by the police, but Steve and Curly were.

'Does he want to see me?' asked Pete.

'Why should he?' said Vince, coldly. 'You wasn't there yesterday. You took good care of that.'

And that was the last anybody said to Pete for the rest of the day. By the end of afternoon school the form had pretty well divided into two factions – the fast-talking ones, who were prepared to admire Vince and Curly and Steve for doing something bold; and the righteous ones who said it served them right to have got caught. Tom by implication was in the second group. Was it not he who had been so keen to catch the 'burglars', and had turned unquestioningly to Pete for help? But he had very little to say on the matter, and nothing at all to Pete.

Pete found himself quite alone, between the two groups; to the rebels, he was the turncoat, and possibly the traitor who had given the show away; to the righteous, he was the one who had shared in the spoils while pretending to be the thief-catcher. Since the headmaster continued not to send for him, he could not even be seen to be paying for his sins.

Then, just as he was leaving the class-room at the end of school, Steve met him.

'Message for you,' said Steve. 'The Head wants to see you before you go for the bus.'

Pete looked quickly up at him, his heart missing a beat, but Steve's face was completely expressionless.

'Me?' he said. 'What about?' It was a stupid thing to say in the circumstances, but Steve looked so casual, as though he were the chance messenger in an affair which was no concern of his, and was already continuing on his way down the corridor. He glanced back over his shoulder at Pete.

'How should I know?' he said, coldly.

'Steve!' said Pete. 'Steve! Tell me!' He was trotting down the corridor after him.

Steve turned then, and looked him up and down with an expression of such scorn that Pete dropped back a step.

'Hoping for your reward, I suppose,' he said. 'Hadn't you better run along and see what it is?' Then he walked off down the corridor among the ebbing tides of schoolchildren.

Pete watched him, hating him. Then he thought, 'I must just tell Tom what has happened, and ask him to keep me a seat,' and at once remembered it wasn't as easy as that. Almost in the same instant, Tom shouldered past him, unspeaking, and disappeared among the crowds. Pete turned and blundered his way up against the flow till he reached the now deserted passage leading to the headmaster's room, and knocked at the door.

At the same time, the door opened from inside, and the school secretary stood in the doorway, her back to Pete, and still carrying on a conversation with the Head. He moved away awkwardly, not sure what he ought to do. She kept on half turning, as though to leave, and then the Head would think of something else.

I shall miss my bus, thought Pete anxiously, but then she saw him.

'There's a boy here,' she remarked to the headmaster. 'I don't know why he's here *now*.' She made it seem as though it were Pete's fault he was still waiting outside. 'Do you want to see him?'

'It's a bit late,' said the Head. 'Who is it?'

'Jenkins, sir,' said Pete. 'Peter Jenkins.' He felt very awkward talking like this to an unseen voice, with the secretary standing in front of him.

'Go on in then,' she said sharply, and Pete went. The Head seemed preoccupied with his papers.

'You sent for me, sir,' said Pete, after a pause, thinking about the bus.

'Yes,' said the Head. 'Jenkins, isn't it? You'll have to be quick, or you'll miss your bus.'

'Yes, sir,' said Pete. And whose fault's that? he thought.

'I understand you were with Vincent Davies helping him keep watch outside Mr Williamson's shop while two older boys went in and stole sweets and money. Is that correct?'

'Yes, sir,' said Pete, startled now that the accusation should come so quick and so unvarnished. Then he tried to collect his thoughts. 'It was only once, sir, and that was sort of by mistake.'

'I fail to see how you can do something like that by mistake,' said the Head. 'Did you have your share of the stolen goods?'

'Only a few sweets, sir.'

'And some cigarettes?'

'Yes, sir.' What use to say only one, and that one he threw away?

'And you knew they were stolen?'

'Yes, sir, but not until afterwards, and it was too late, then.'

The headmaster was not impressed by this, or just was not listening. He said a short piece about stealing and the good name of the school. Pete found it hard to concentrate on what he was saying, because half his mind was on the unfairness of the situation, and half was on the school bus. Out of the tail of his eye he could see several of the buses moving off up the road, and wondered how long his would wait for him.

'I hope you are listening to me, Jenkins.'

'Yes, sir.'

'I understand that you are one of two reserves to go on the school trip to Germany.'

'Yes, I was going, but then there were two places short, but now Mr Turner says I can go after all because somebody has dropped out.'

'Then I shall inform Mr Turner that the vacancy should be offered to the other reserve. In the circumstances, you can hardly expect me to allow you to go, and I am sure when Mr Turner learns about the situation he will agree with me. We do not want our school to be represented abroad by a gang of shop-lifters.'

Pete stared at him blankly for a moment, as the truth sank in. Yet what sort of truth was this?

'Please, sir,' he began, 'it wasn't like that. I know it sounds bad, but . . .'

'I don't want to hear any more about it,' said the Head. 'You must not keep your bus waiting any longer. I will write a note in the morning to your father, and he can come and see me if he likes.'

'My father is working away, up in Scotland.'

'Well, your mother then. Has she paid the full amount for the trip?'

'Only twenty-five pounds. She'll be giving me the rest on Tuesday – tomorrow.'

'Then you can let her know there is no necessity for that, and I will be handing back the twenty-five direct to her when she comes to see me. Now hurry up and get your bus.' The Head started to look at his papers again, and Pete turned dispiritedly away.

He ran out across the yard to where the one remaining bus stood ready to go, the engine running.

'Nearly missed it that time,' said the driver, cheerfully, and swung off up the road.

Pete glanced round for the empty space by Tom, but Tom was sharing a seat with a solid small boy who lived two miles out of town, and staring steadily out of the window away from him. Pete sat down in the vacant seat behind, and when the small boy got off, he leaned over to speak to Tom.

'Shall I come over?' he said, trying to make his voice sound casual. Normally he would just have moved in without asking.

'No, thanks,' said Tom. They were the only words he had spoken since morning assembly.

Pete sat back in silence. As he stared out at the sunny countryside the familiar fields grew blurred in front of his eyes.

When he got home, he said nothing straightaway to his mother about what had happened; he had no particular purpose in mind, but he could not face another scene. It was only later, sitting on the shingle by the stream at the end of the field, that the idea had come to him.

He had gone down there for somewhere to think where his mother would not see him moping around and ask questions. There was thunder in the air after the spell of fine weather, and the midges hung in a cloud over the water. Every now and again a swallow darted low along the stream between the trees, but otherwise the birds were unnaturally still, waiting for big drops of rain to begin falling. He picked up an oval pebble and weighed it in his hand, feeling the solid smoothness of it, then lay back against a tree-trunk, turning his head to rub his cheek against the warm rough bark. There was some comfort in these things, but they did not reach to the ache in his heart.

'When I go home,' he thought, 'I'll have to tell Mum, and then go through all that business all over again.' He sighed. Then the idea came to him. What if he said nothing about the trip being off, but just took the ten pounds she was due to give him in the morning and went away somewhere on his own for the fortnight that the school visit was due to last? He could go and see his father after all. He would enjoy that. And he would go to a football match – the one in Cardiff Vince was telling him about. Ten pounds was not much to live on for a fortnight, but his grandmother had promised him some pocket-money for the trip, and once he got to Kell his father would look after him, and bring him back on his next trip home. At least, he hoped he would. He was not actually so worried about his father's reaction as he was about his mother's, when the truth eventually came out, as it must; Kell was a long way away, a different land, make-believe, even; but home and school were near and real, and that was where his mother would first find out the truth, either from Tom's family, or when she visited the Head – but by then he would be safely in Scotland. What happened when he arrived home was something to be faced when the time came, but in his present mood he almost welcomed the thought of a show-down with someone, and his mother would do as well as anyone. And Uncle Sam, the interfering old fellow. At the back of his mind Pete knew that neither his mother nor his uncle had done anything at all to deserve these harsh thoughts about them, but he derived a kind of savage satisfaction out of imagining how prejudiced and unsympathetic they would be. That way, he did not feel so guilty about deceiving them.

In fact, he told himself, he was glad, glad that he was not to be able to go on the school trip; it was a great piece of luck, making it possible for him to fulfil his two dearest ambitions, ambitions his mother had always thwarted, of going to a football match and going to stay with his father. He overlooked the fact that he had only himself thought of visiting his father for the first time a bare week ago.

He sat there by the stream, happily dreaming of the crowded stadium and the waving cheering crowds, himself among them, holding his scarf stretched out between his hands high above his head; he saw himself walking up the great new road on Kell to where a group of men were working. 'Hullo, Dad,' he'd say, and the tall man at the centre of the group would turn, and as recognition dawned on his face he would smile slowly, and say, 'Why, it's our Pete!'

He got up eventually, and walked quietly home in the July dusk, wrapped in the protective armour of his secret adventure.

When he got to bed that night he began to realize that there were a good many practical difficulties to overcome. For instance, how was he going to get away from home without his mother discovering he was not travelling with the school party? The arrangement was that the members of the group went to school as usual on Friday, taking their suitcases with them, and they all set out together on a coach to catch a train to London and then on to Harwich. Pete himself would have to keep out of the way from the end of school on Friday – he could not slip off from school earlier because the school authorities, knowing he was not going on the trip, would notice his absence and make inquiries. On the other hand, he could not go back home that night because his mother would assume he was on the night boat to Germany by then. If he was going to try and hitch-hike to Cardiff, and there would be no other way of getting there on Friday after four o'clock in the afternoon, he would be faced with the problem of having to spend the night either on the way, or else after arriving late in a strange city.

Then there was the problem of his suitcase. His mother, of course, would want to check that he had all the right things for Germany in it, and would expect to see him off for the bus with the suitcase in his hand. Tom, on the other hand, and the other children on the bus, would expect him to be carrying only his usual school satchel; Pete could see a most embarrassing situation arising. He considered the possibility of taking Tom into his confidence, but discarded the idea. The only way was to make sure his mother did not go beyond the garden gate to see him off, and somehow to hide his suitcase and collect his satchel before the bus came. Then, later, he would have to retrieve his suitcase because he would need it for his own adventure.

These were the first problems to be faced and so they loomed larger; but beyond them lurked others – finding somewhere to spend not just Friday night but every night until he joined his father, making his way to Scotland and to Kell on his small sum of money, and all the time avoiding any suspicion that he might be a boy on the run. Many times between that first Friday evening and the moment of departure Pete decided to abandon the whole scheme, but each time he was afraid to go and tell his mother, not just that the trip was off, but why. When the Head gave him a note asking his mother to go and see him as soon as possible, Pete destroyed it and just told her that he would like her to call and see him on the last Friday of term – that would be a week after Pete had gone, and he could write before then and make his own explanation. The Head obviously thought Pete's mother was not trying very hard when Pete told him this was the only day she could manage, but there was not much he could do about it.

Pete's mother had a letter on Wednesday that made him even more determined to stick to his plan. She and Uncle Sam had a sister who had married a college lecturer and lived in the United States with their family of two girls and a boy. Once, two years ago, they had spent the summer at Llanwern, and Pete had found his cousins very tiresome company. Moreover, in order that they could all stay in his mother's house, Pete had been farmed out with Uncle Sam by night, while spending the days in his own over-crowded home without a room he could call his own. Now his aunt had written to confirm that they were coming again, and arriving on Saturday for a fortnight.

'What a pity,' said his mother, when she read the letter. 'It will be just the time you are away and they'll scarcely see anything of you.'

'It'll make more room,' said Pete.

'That's no problem,' said Mrs Jenkins. 'Uncle Sam is always pleased to put you up, and your aunty's family like to be all together here anyway. But it's a shame you won't have a chance to play with your cousins. You get little enough opportunity to get to know each other as it is.'

Pete did not exactly dislike his cousins; it was just that they had nothing in common. The oldest girl, who was the same age as Pete, he remembered, was very clever – so clever she did not boast about it, or show off about knowing more than Pete, but was tactful and modest and tried to talk to him only about things he knew of; it made Pete feel a bit like Aunt Emmy. The next one, who was two years younger, was more of a show-off, and they were always quarrelling, and the youngest, who was the only boy, was a bit of a mother's baby; he wasn't someone you could rag about with like Gary or Jimmy Price or even Fish. Pete decided he was much better off out of the way. The only trouble was, he did not really want the storm to break about his escapade while the American cousins were there, but that was something which could not be helped.

'You're very quiet these days,' his mother remarked suddenly. 'Are you worried about being away from home for so long?'

'Of course not,' said Pete, in genuine surprise.

'They'll look after you,' his mother went on comfortably. 'That master – he's taken these parties before, hasn't he? I remember Mrs Thomas told me Linda went a couple of years ago, and everything was very well organized.'

'Too well if you ask me,' said Pete, absently.

'And I've got this for you,' said his mother. She handed him a bundle of notes. Pete looked at them in silence. 'There's five there – your Grandad gave them to me for you.'

Pete looked up. 'From Grandad?'

'He said it was for you to spend on what you wanted,' she said. 'Nana said as you ought to have money in your pockets same as the other boys.'

'Yeah,' said Pete. He knew he ought to say more, but his tongue would not say it. 'Ta,' he managed to mutter at last.

His mother looked at him sharply. 'That's not much thanks,' she commented. 'You've not even been near the place for weeks. It wouldn't cost you much to slip up there this evening on your bike and say thank you.'

'I'll do that,' said Pete. It would be nice to get away. 'I'll go up straightaway.' He stood silent, fiddling with the notes in his hand. 'I'm – I'm sorry,' he said suddenly. Sorry for a whole lot of things, he thought, yet not sorry enough to tell her what they all were.

She suddenly put her arm round him – something she rarely did nowadays.

'You'll be all right,' she said. 'It's me that'll be worrying. I shall miss you, Pete. D'you know that? Be sure and send me lots of postcards.'

Pete nodded. 'Sure,' he said, and turned away quickly.

Postcards. That was something he had not thought about. Could he take Tom into his confidence after all, and get him to send a postcard to his mother? He had not spoken to Tom all week, and the longer they went on not talking the higher grew the wall of silence between them. In any case, Pete wrote rather neatly but Tom had a scrawly hand; Mum would be bound to notice the difference. Perhaps he should leave a note in his bedroom for her to find and open after he had gone – but the trouble with that was that if he left it in an obvious place she might very well go into his room and find it during the day while he was still at school, and if he hid it away a bit she might not find it at all.

Eventually he decided the best thing would be to write his postcard from Scotland telling her the truth; that way he could own up from a safe distance and give her time to get used to the idea before she could get at him.

On Thursday night, Pete lay in bed gazing wide-eyed at the dusky summer night sky, wishing he had never thought of the mad scheme. It was not the first time he had felt that way, but never before had the difficulties loomed so alarmingly or the consequences to his relations with his mother and the rest of his family seemed so grave. What would Mum think when she got his letter? How would she feel? Would she ever forgive him?

At one stage he nearly got out of bed to go and tell her the whole truth – but then as he got one bare foot to the cold linoleum he remembered Auntie Sybil's visit. To Pete Auntie Sybil was a comparative stranger, but he knew his mother felt differently about her. She would tell Auntie Sybil things in the way that she would tell Uncle Sam – things she would not think of discussing with other grown-ups, and things, especially, about Pete. If he went now and told his mother the whole story about Bongo's and the school trip, he knew she would pretend to the neighbours that she had known all along, but before twenty-four hours had passed she would be pouring the whole affair out to Auntie Sybil, who in her turn would tell Uncle Don, and soon it would be a family scandal, and from there a casual reference by one of the girls would have it common knowledge all over the village.

Pete curled back under the bed-clothes. No, he would have to go through with it now, and make a success of it.

He slept very restlessly that night. Sometimes he found his mind going over all the details while he was wide awake and thinking things out sensibly; then it would do it all over again when he was half-asleep, and all kinds of unforeseen disasters crept in, and his half-waking brain struggled to cope with these without realizing they were only dream-disasters. He spent the night endlessly looking for his suitcase which was not where he had hidden it; and seeing his mother trudging inexorably up the village street to the spot where the school bus stopped, although he had already said good-bye to her at the garden gate, and he was standing there waiting with Tom and his parents, praying the bus would come and go before his mother reached him. The bus indeed came into sight, but the whole scene went into slow motion, the bus always approaching but never arriving, his mother getting nearer and nearer. Then a deeper sleep overtook him, but he woke in the middle of a much more terrifying nightmare. He was standing at the front of the crowds round the football ground, and the mass of huge men behind him kept pressing, pressing upon him till he could not breathe and he knew that either his ribs must crack or the wodden barrier on which he was leaning; and at last it went, slowly, with a strange long-drawn-out metallic sound, and he was falling, falling, with this terrible weight behind him.

Then he dropped back into his own body comfortably sprawled in bed, and the alarm clock was singing out from his mother's bedroom.

As the meaning of the day sank in, he lay gripped by panic for a brief moment. Then he got resolutely up, and as soon as he began to dress he felt quite different, detached, business-like and unconcerned.

The mood lasted all through the school day. The big moment of get-away went off without a hitch, and that gave his confidence a great boost. His mother said good-bye to him in the house; although she felt his going keenly, it did not occur to her that she might do anything as unexpected as walking down to the bus with him. She made sure he had his suitcase and his money and all his papers – most of those were kept by Coot anyway – and kissed him in the kitchen.

'Write to me, won't you?' she said.

'Yeah, sure,' said Pete, and let himself out of the front door.

He was in good time. He ran quickly round to the back garden, out into the field and down along the hedge to the stream. There he slipped his suitcase into a hollow tree he knew about, and collected the satchel he had hidden the night before. Then he walked up the short-cut that ran by the stream to rejoin the main road by the bridge at the bottom of the village. Luckily no one was about to see him walking up the road to the shop, which was where the bus stopped and which lay between his house and the bridge. It seemed an awful long wait there, shouldering the tell-tale satchel full of school books instead of a travelling suitcase, and he was in constant fear that Uncle Sam would emerge from his house just up the road to see him off. He had gone round there last night to say good-bye but one could not be sure. At last the bus came and Pete climbed on. Sam must have been keeping an eye open for it, because he came to his door then and waved. Pete waved happily back, his belongings safely stowed away in the rack above his head.

There was an embarrassing moment, though not a dangerous one, when Tom got on a little farther up the road, at the cross-roads by his farm. His father was there, and he came up on to the step of the bus in order to speak to Pete, who was sitting very quiet hoping not to be noticed.

'I'm ever so sorry to hear you can't go after all,' he said to him kindly. 'Tom never said till just now, I don't know why.'

'Can't be helped,' said Pete, awkwardly.

'Tell you what,' said Mr Thomas. 'Kevin is taking some stock to Hereford on Saturday. If you would like to go with him I'm sure he'd be glad of your help.'

'Thank you very much,' said Pete, wondering how to get out of that one. Then a happy thought struck him. 'But my auntie from America is arriving tomorrow, and I expect Mum would want me at home.'

'Sybil?' said Mr Thomas with a big smile. 'You tell her to come right on up and see us as soon as she can spare the time. We used to sit together in the class, Sybil and me.' He would have gone on talking, but the bus had to go, so he said good-bye to Tom and backed down into the lane, pulling the heavy door across as he did so.

Tom had been standing awkwardly in the middle of the aisle while his father was talking, knowing Mr Thomas would assume he was going to sit with Pete, though in fact he had not done so all week. Now as the bus lurched on, he hesitated a moment and then slid into his accustomed seat beside his friend. Pete was looking steadily out of the window, but half turned as he felt Tom join him.

'Shall I?' asked Tom.

'Yeah, if you want to.' Pete continued to look out of the window.

'I'm sorry you aren't coming,' said Tom, after a pause.

'I'll think of you if there's a howling gale tonight,' Pete replied.

'Thanks,' said Tom. 'You know that extra place?' he went on after a pause. 'Why did Sally Price get it and not you? You were above her on the list.'

'Yeah,' said Pete. 'I know. The Head said I wasn't to go.'

There was a long pause.

'Was that because of Bongo's?' said Tom at last.

'Yeah,' said Pete.

'But that wasn't fair. You scarcely had anything to do with it.'

'I know,' said Pete. 'But he thought I did, and so,' he added bitterly, 'did most people, come to that.' He kept weaving the strap of his satchel between his restless fingers.

'Why didn't you *tell* me?' said Tom. 'You never said nothing, so of course I thought you was in it from the start. It was only yesterday when Vince was talking about it that I knew any different.'

'I didn't think you wanted to know,' said Pete. He slipped his fingers from the loops and carefully flattened the strap across his knees. He felt suddenly relaxed and comfortable again.

'Vince is O.K.,' said Tom. 'Like I said he's a daft nit, but he's O.K. really. Does your mum know why you're not going?'

'Not yet,' said Pete. He drew a deep breath. 'I've got my own plans . . .' he began, but then the bus pulled up and a couple of girls got into the seat in front of them, and immediately leant over the back of the seat and began a conversation.

There was no chance to say any more before they got to school, but the wall was down. Pete was glad of that; he felt happier about taking off on his own adventures now things were going to be all right between Tom and him. If there had been an opportunity he would have told Tom about his plans, but almost as soon as they got to school the party for Germany was marshalled into their coach and disappeared.

Pete's next hazardous moment came at the end of school. Now he had to go back on the bus, get off at his usual spot and out of the village with his suitcase, without being seen. Then he remembered he need not get off at the shop; it being Friday, his mother would be up at his grandparents', and it was the day he often got off at the cross-roads and had tea with Tom. Admittedly Tom was not on the bus this afternoon, but Pete could still be having tea at Tygwyn for all the driver or the other children knew.

As they approached the cross-roads, Pete slipped up the aisle and spoke to the driver, who nodded without turning his head, and slowed to a halt. Pete jumped off and watched the bus disappearing down the road. Then he ran down the Tygwyn lane as far as the gate into the field on the right, climbed over and loped along under the hedge, keeping a sharp look-out for any of the Thomases. He reached the stream well below the shingle patch, but that was better than cutting boldly across the middle of the field, for alders grew along the stream banks and it was easy to make his way along unnoticed. When he got to the hollow tree he took out the suitcase and removed some of the tidy clothes his mother had thought fit to pack, and stuffed them in his satchel. Then he cut back under the other hedgerow to his own back garden.

Pete turned in through the gate, hoping his mother had not come home early in order to get ready for Auntie Sybil. All was quiet, so he slipped in and up to his bedroom. Here he took off his school uniform and stowed it away at the bottom of his private tea chest, where he kept all his own belongings, together with the best clothes. He knew it would be no use putting them in his drawers because his mother would be emptying them out for the visitors. Then he put on some old clothes and an anorak and was just about to run downstairs when he realized he had left the whole of his fifteen pounds in his top blazer pocket. All day he had been conscious of carrying so much money around with him in school, but now, of all times, he had nearly forgotten it. Quickly he burrowed down to the bottom of the tea-chest and extracted them, counting them nervously as he made his way downstairs.

Just then it occurred to him that his duffle bag would be much more use to him than a smart borrowed suitcase on the kind of journey he proposed to make, so he went into the back kitchen to collect it.

It was while he was in there that he heard the front door opening. His mother *had* come home early.

For a moment Pete stood panic-stricken. To get out of the house he had to go through into the kitchen proper and so out of the back door, but he would not have time to do that before his mother came straight through from the front. Even as he realized this, he heard her come into the kitchen and set her heavy basket on the table. Pete hoped he had not left anything lying about. He had, however, left the back door open, and he heard his mother give a surprised exclamation as she noticed this. Then she walked over and shut it.

Pete felt trapped. She walked over to the sink, filled a kettle and put it on the stove. At any moment now she might come into the back kitchen for something – it was little more than a cupboard, but everything was kept in it that did not have a place anywhere else in the house. Instead, however, she went back up the little corridor, and the next moment Pete heard her trudging up the stairs.

Now was his moment. He crept out, across the kitchen, opened the back door with enormous care and made himself close it equally carefully behind him. Then he paused. If his mother went into his bedroom, she would have a clear view out of his window over the back garden, and, if she looked out, would see him scampering down the garden to the gate into the field. On the other hand, she was more likely to go to her own bedroom first, which looked out over the village street, to change her shoes, in which case now was the moment to seize. Even if she were in his room, he reflected, she would not be likely to be looking out of the window when there was work to be done. Pete took a deep breath and ran down to the gate and slipped through.

Standing screened by the hawthorn hedge he peered back at the house. All was absolutely still. He heaved a sigh of relief, and made his way once more down to the stream. Sitting on the shingle in his own private world, he opened the suitcase and packed the contents into the duffle. Then he wondered what to do with the suitcase. It actually belonged to Mrs Burns, of the village shop, and had been lent for the occasion. He wondered if Mrs Burns would approve of her suitcase being stored in a hollow tree for a fortnight, and decided she would have to put up with it. Then he thought of Bottom Barn. This was an old stone barn near the stream, belonging to Mr Thomas, and now newly-filled with the season's hay. He ran along to the barn with the suitcase and threw it up on top of the sweet-smelling bales. This was where Fish had hidden for nights on end last winter with his dog, Floss, when he was suspected of sheep-killing. It was a dry, cosy, place. For a moment Pete toyed with the idea of spending the night right here, and starting for Cardiff first thing in the morning. One thing prevented him, however, and that was hunger. He had not thought to lay in any food, meaning to buy it on the way; that being so, the sooner he got far enough from home to buy food safely, the better.

He left the barn, went back and picked up the duffle bag, and started walking upstream. Very soon he would reach the bridge at the end of the village, but he knew he must cross the stream before then and cut through a plantation to give himself plenty of cover, and avoid coming out until he was at least two miles clear of the village, and well past his grandfather's cottage, which lay on the road he had to take.

He managed to achieve all this successfully – the stream was low at that time of year and easy to ford – but by the time he judged it safe to come out on the main road and start looking for lifts it was six o'clock. All day Peter had been too nervous to eat, and now he was starving. He heard the slow rumble of a heavy vehicle coming up the hill towards him, hidden round the bend. He stuck his arm boldly out into the road and jerked his thumb in the direction of Cardiff, seventy miles away.

Chapter 5

THE lorry driver gave him a lift as far as Merthyr Tydfil. That was where he lived, but he told Pete he could easily catch a bus from there to Cardiff, and he dropped him by the bus station. This suited Pete fine, because there was a refreshment place open where, at last, he could fill his aching void. However, time was getting on, and if he was too late arriving in Cardiff he would have trouble finding a place for the night without arousing suspicion that he was on the run. Besides, he did not fancy being homeless and lost in a strange city in the dark. So he went to the ticket office first, discovered that a bus was leaving for Cardiff in twenty minutes, and then went back to the café and bought himself a plateful of sausages and chips. The place was moderately full, so Pete sat down at a table where two stout ladies were talking over a cup of coffee on the opposite side. He did not pay them much attention, because his whole mind was set on finishing his meal before catching the bus. Out of the tail of his eye he saw the two ladies casting amused looks at his fast-emptying plate, and then at each other, but he did not bother much about that, and a moment later they both got up, still talking, and walked off towards the buses.

Pete decided he was still not nearly full enough for comfort, so he went back to the counter and bought two cheese sandwiches, a packet of crisps, two chocolate wafer biscuits and a bottle of pop. He stuffed these in the top of his duffle bag, and ran off to catch the bus. He found an empty seat half-way down the bus, and two minutes later they were off.

Pete was surprised to find, after paying for his ticket and his food, that out of a whole pound note he only had five pence change. It seemed a lot for one meal and a short bus ride – he could have a fortnight's school meals for that. However, he still had fourteen pounds left, and once he got to Kell everything would be all right.

It was as he bit into his second sandwich that he heard a familiar laugh, and glancing sideways realized that the same two stout ladies who had sat opposite him in the café were now in the seat immediately across the aisle.

'Reminds me of my sister's boy, Alan,' he overheard one of them say. 'Great one for his meals, Alan is, yet he don't never seem to get any flesh on him. I said to Nancy – my sister you know – only the other day; well, how do you keep him fed, I said ...'

The interminable chat went on. If Pete felt the occasional amused look cast in his direction, he paid no attention. He was hungry.

As they drew nearer to Cardiff the roadside villages clustered more thickly until they formed a continuous ribbon of terraced roofs and industrial estates. One of the stout ladies got off, with all her packages clasped around her.

'So long, Beth,' she said. 'I shall be looking for you on Monday.'

'I'll be there, don't you worry. Look after yourself.'

'Tara. Give my love to Bert.' And with a lot more laughter, she was gone.

The remaining one glanced around brightly, and smiled at Pete, as though reluctant to settle for her own company. He gave her a cautious grin and went on stolidly eating crisps. She had bright black hair and bright black eyes and the rolls of fat around her jaw were never in repose because her lips were forever ready to break into a smile. When she spoke, her voice was louder and more lilting than Pete was accustomed to.

'Feeling better now?' she asked merrily, as Pete licked his fingers after finishing his crisps and got out the bottle of pop. He nodded, and took a swig.

'Hungry, weren't you?' she persisted.

'Yeah.' It did not sound very forthcoming, but it would have taken more than that to have daunted her. She talked away, and the occasional grunt or 'yes' seemed to satisfy her very well.

After a bit she began to ask questions. Did he live in Cardiff, where was he going to, how old was he, what family had he, and so on. It was just lively nosiness, and Pete was quite glad to have a chance to try out his story. He had decided to stick to the truth as far as possible, because it was easier and he had heard on some television programme that it was the best thing to do. He told her that he was travelling to Cardiff to catch a train to Scotland where he was meeting his father. He had missed an earlier bus and now he would have to spend the night in Cardiff, and did not quite know how to set about it. That was all true enough.

The lady looked at him consideringly. 'Have you got a mother, bach, or is she dead?'

Pete thought about this. It might be fun to be an orphan, but if he killed off his mother he would have to invent a substitute.

'No, she's fine,' he said. 'She would have come with me to Cardiff only she had to go up to my grandparents. They've took ill.' The lady's benign interest was boundless. He had to tell her all about the grandparents, and Aunt Emmy – by the time he had exaggerated their troubles to create a crisis they all sounded bed-ridden, certifiable or practically dying – but he began to be thankful he wasn't relying entirely on his imagination, because it would have run out long before the lady's curiosity. He fed her with Uncle Sam, and Auntie Sybil, and Tom and school, and even touched on the school trip, but cautiously.

'To Germany, it is,' he said.

'Why aren't you going then, love?'

'Couldn't afford it,' said Pete. 'After, Mum did think she could manage, but by then there weren't no places.'

The black-haired lady clucked sympathetically. 'Better luck next year,' she said. 'And now you're off to visit your father instead, so you're all right, aren't you?'

Pete nodded and said nothing. He felt he was getting on dangerous ground. However, her next words really got him scared.

'What school do you go to, bach?' she asked. 'My sister, Nancy, the one I was talking about just now, she's got relatives up in Mid-Wales and I think she said their boy – her nephew, that would be – is off to Germany on a school trip.'

'I don't expect it's the same one,' said Pete hurriedly. 'Lots of schools go to Germany.'

'You never know,' said the lady. 'I can't recall the name. Would it be Llandovery?'

'Very like,' said Pete, relieved. 'Aberafon school, I go to.'

'It could be,' said the lady. 'Now I come to think of it, it's the name of the village where these people have a farm I'm thinking of, not the school. It's Llan-something, that I do know. Mind you, there's a lot of them around.'

'Yeah,' said Pete, shortly. He wished she would leave it alone, but she wouldn't.

'They're not really my relatives, see,' she explained. 'It's my sister's husband's people; his sister it is, married a farmer up in those parts. Quite a big noise, I fancy. County Councillor and that, so my sister says. Myfanwy, her sister-in-law is, Myfanwy . . . Thomas, that's it. Married a John Thomas. Got four or five children, I believe, and it's one of them what is going on this trip. My sister did say his name, but I forget now. Would it be Tom? Tom Thomas?'

All through this chat, Pete was getting more and more alarmed. What should he say? He knew if he denied all knowledge, she wasn't one to let the matter drop, and he would have to be awfully careful not to get caught out.

'Could be,' he said cautiously.

'Aberafon,' she murmured to herself. She was as keen a listener as she was a talker. 'Could be the place. I'll tell you what, though. Of course you'll know all about it, living in those parts. That village, Llan-something, it was in the news last year when a boy got lost, ran off with his sheepdog or something. They found him in the end, I remember, but there was quite a rumpus at the time. You'll know what I'm talking about.'

Pete knew all right. That would have been Fish, when his dog, Floss, was suspected of killing sheep. Pete knew all about that, and of course Uncle Sam had been in the thick of it.

'Hey,' she said suddenly, 'didn't you say your friend's name was Tom?'

'That's right,' said Pete. Cornered, he decided the only thing was to brazen it out. After all, the connection between this woman and the Thomases wasn't all that close; there was not really any harm in letting her know that Tom was his friend.

She was thrilled at the discovery, and talked away, asking him all about Fish and that episode with Floss, and all about the Thomas family.

'My sister Nance will be interested,' she said. 'Tom's been to stay with her – at least I think that must be the one. He'd be a bit younger than her boy, Alan – Tom's cousin, he'd be.'

Alan, thought Pete. The nephew who ate so much and never put on flesh. He must be the admired cousin Tom was always talking about. Tom had said he was small for his age.

The lady leant across and tapped him on the knee.

'I'll be getting off in a couple of minutes,' she said, 'and that's where you'll be getting off, too. I take in lodgers, but I've only got the one just now and there's the spare bedroom going a-begging. You come to our place tonight, and I'll see you're all right. You don't need to worry about payment, now. I'll be glad for you to come, and know you're safe and properly looked after.'

Pete paused. He felt uneasy now she knew so much about him, but on the other hand it was only for one night, and it would look odd if he refused. She was kind, too. He decided to risk it.

'Oh, thanks,' he said. 'I've got money, though, for the journey, what Mum gave me. She wouldn't like it if I didn't pay for my lodgings.'

'Oh, well, love, you do as you please. We'll talk about it in the morning. Help me with this old basket, there's a good boy. We get off just at the corner there.'

She swept him off and up to her trim semi-detached house, introduced him to a small grey husband in shirt-sleeves, sat him down in front of the television and brought him a steaming mug of Horlicks. Then she showed him up to a bedroom with a thick fitted carpet and a bed hiding under a bulging satin wine-coloured quilt.

'One thing, love; do you think you should ring your mother and say you're all right?'

'She's not on the phone,' said Pete with relief. 'Anyway, she doesn't know I missed the bus, so she won't be worrying.'

'What about your dad, then? I suppose you were meant to be catching the night train to Glasgow. Will he be meeting the train in the morning?'

Pete had a brain-wave. 'No, I was to ring him when I got there, and he would tell me where to meet him then. He wasn't sure which day I was coming.'

'That was lucky.' She drew his curtains and turned back the sheet. 'Then we can ring the station tomorrow morning, no doubt, and ask when there's another train. Or will you wait and go on the night train tomorrow evening?'

That sounded a splendid idea. It would take care of where to spend tomorrow night, and save arriving in another strange city at nightfall. Up to this moment he had not the slightest idea of how to set about getting from Cardiff to Scotland, but this seemed too easy. He said boldly, 'If I did that, I'd be able to go to the football match at Ninian Park tomorrow afternoon, wouldn't I?'

She looked at him then, a slow grin spreading itself among the rolls of fat. 'You were pretty lucky, missing that bus, weren't you?' She shook her head and laughed aloud. 'Tell me – was it really an accident?'

'I never said it were an accident,' said Pete innocently.

'No, you never,' crowed his landlady, slapping a fat thigh. 'Boys! I don't know what your mother's thinking about, letting you loose on the world, a wild one like you. But maybe she's right. I'd say you can look after yourself all right. You've got to learn.' She went to the door. 'Time you was in bed. I'll give you a call at eight-thirty. Sleep tight, and God bless.'

'Good night,' said Pete. He was soon in that cosy bed, and slept dreamlessly till woken by her cheery voice in the morning.

By then Pete had ceased to worry about the danger of being found out. His landlady was inquisitive and talkative but not at all suspicious, and there seemed no reason, when he thought about it quietly, why she should try and get in touch with the Thomases in Llanwern. After all, she did not even know them herself.

He had, however, reckoned without her kind intentions. She came into the dining-room where Pete was wading through a plate piled high with bacon and egg, beaming.

'I've just been on to my sister Nance on the phone,' she announced. 'I felt pretty sure that if there was a football match on this afternoon her boy Alan would be going. Mad on football, he is. I thought it would be such a pity, you going along all on your own, and your first match, I dare say; but it's all right, I've got it all fixed up. Alan is going, he's coming into town with some of his friends – they live out at Pendinas, a few miles out, that is – and I've told him you'll meet them by the traffic lights at the corner of the Castle. I'll tell you how to get there, and you can't miss it. Then you can all have a meal together at the snack bar or somewhere, before going along to Ninian Park. That'll be much nicer for you than going all on your own.'

'You've gone to a lot of trouble,' said Pete, weakly, after a pause.

'It's no trouble, love, that's just the way I am,' said the landlady with candour. 'You don't want to do things all on your own when you can have company. I love a bit of company, I do.'

Pete stuffed his mouth very full to avoid having to speak for some time, and thought furiously. Should he make up some reason for not joining Alan? He couldn't think of anything convincing. Should he just not turn up at the meeting-place? But then he would either have to forgo the football match, or else spend the whole afternoon trying to avoid likely-looking groups of boys. Besides, what harm could it do? It would be rather nice, when Tom came back from Germany and started talking about the visit of his cousin Alan, to be able to say he had been to a football match with him. He would not need to sit around waiting for Tom to introduce him to his cousin. And Pete was curious to know what he was really like, this cousin of Tom's.

After breakfast his landlady gave him detailed instructions as to how to get to the Castle, and said good-bye fondly. She said he would not have time to come back out to the suburbs of Cardiff between the end of the football match and catching the night train, but she urged him to come and see her again next time he was in Cardiff. She quite refused to take any money off him. 'After all, you're my relative really, aren't you?' she said. 'Or almost.'

Pete couldn't quite see how she worked that one out, and he had a feeling his mother would not approve of his cadging a free night's lodging. All the same, he had spent one of his fifteen pounds already, and could scarcely be said to have started his journey to Kell as yet, so he was glad to give in; in any case she so enjoyed being kind it seemed churlish to refuse her.

So, at noon, Pete was sitting on a low wall outside Cardiff Castle, eating an ice-cream as he waited for Alan and his friends. To his right, the brightly-coloured traffic ground along the shopping streets, pausing at the changing lights with a monstrous sighing of air-brakes on the big articulated lorries, the sports cars revving away again with a squeal of tyres on the hot and shiny tarmac. Near him the thick cord of vehicles frayed out and sped away from the knotted centre, north and west and east. In front, parked cars nibbled round the edges of the green oases that separated the dignified white buildings of the city centre, like a plague of ladybirds. Occasionally one ladybird would wriggle out backwards and zoom off up the street, but its place would very soon be taken by another, circling round looking for just such an opportunity.

The sun was warm, and everything had gone to plan. Here he was, proved to be perfectly capable of looking after himself, only a short distance away from his first football match. And after? Well, he had achieved one journey and one overnight stay without any trouble, so there was no reason why he should not go on doing so.

The approaching meeting with Alan added piquancy to the situation. True, there was an element of danger – Pete would have to be on his guard not to give the show away – but only enough to amuse him, not enough to frighten him. When he had thought that he would first meet Alan through Tom, at Tom's house, he had felt certain he would dislike him. Now that he was going to discover him for himself, and unknown to Tom, he was not so sure.

Then he saw them – a group of four boys standing by the traffic lights, looking around. Pete stood up slowly, suddenly shy; at once the smallest boy in the group saw him and, beckoning to the others, came straight over. He was a little dark boy and though he was as skinny as the landlady had been plump, there was something about his bright dark eyes and his outgoing manner that reminded Pete of her. Perhaps this was a small brother of Alan's; he glanced at the other three boys to see if any of them looked like a brother. But by then the small boy was speaking to him.

'Are you Peter Jenkins?' he asked. 'Do you know my cousin Tom?'

'That's right,' said Pete, uncertainly. He looked across at the other boys, all as hesitant and uncertain as he.

'Great,' said the small boy. 'This is Bill, and that's Meirion, and the ginger one's Glyn. They're all friends of mine. My name's Alan.'

'Hi,' said Pete. He looked again at the small dark boy. Tom had said his cousin was small, but Pete had not expected him to be someone he would look down on. He could hardly believe he was fourteen.

'Come on, then, boys,' said Alan. 'Where shall we eat, then? Henry's?'

'Do fine,' said Meirion.

'Let's make it the Corner Café,' said the fair one, called Bill.

'Too far,' said Meirion.

'They do smashing chips,' said Bill.

'What do you say, Glyn?' asked Alan.

'Doesn't worry me,' said Glyn. 'So long as we get there quick. I'm starved.'

'Henry's then,' said Alan, and they all followed him, across the road from the Castle and into the shopping centre.

Pete relaxed. Alan was much less formidable than he had expected. He seemed nice enough, too, friendly and unassuming; not at all the type Tom had led him to expect. It was funny, though, Pete realized after a while, how smoothly everything went under Alan's charge. Usually with a gang of boys out on their own, plans only evolved after a lot of indecision and wrangling, but today it was different. While they walked to Henry's and joined the queue at the self-service counter Alan chatted to Pete about the afternoon's plans, and about football in general. Then he turned to the large menu stuck on the wall.

'What are you going to have?' he asked. 'Pie and chips is best if you're hungry and can't afford a lot. The mixed grill is smashing, but it's awful dear. I have it when I'm feeling rich, but I think I'll just have pie today.'

That made Pete feel easier in his mind. He was beginning to be conscious of the need to eke out his money very carefully if he was to get to Kell on it. Like Alan, he ordered pie. Glyn did the same, but Bill was having problems.

'You can't have baked beans *and* chips with your sausage, dear,' said the assistant.

'Why not?' asked Bill.

'It's one or the other, see?' said the girl. She began to look impatient. 'You can have apple pie to fill up for afters.'

'I don't want apple pie,' muttered Bill. 'Just sausage and chips, then,' he said sadly.

'*And* you want a baked beans on toast,' said Alan. Bill looked blank. 'Separately, I mean. For the boy who's keeping our table.'

'What boy?' said Bill.

'Oh, never mind,' said Alan. 'He wants one sausage and chips and one baked beans on toast, please. Hurry up, Bill, you're keeping everyone waiting. Ta.'

'Who's this for then?' asked Bill, joining him at the pay desk. He looked thoroughly confused.

'You, of course. It's what you wanted, isn't it? I'll have the toast if you don't want it. Just because you can't have it together, there's no law against having it separately. You don't pay for the plate.'

It was obvious when you thought about it. Alan was like that. He did not boss the others around but, as with the choice of eating-place, when he had discovered what they wanted he arranged things without fuss, so that they got it.

He also made Pete feel one of the group. He did not, to Pete's relief, seem particularly curious about his home life and his relations with Tom – no doubt his aunt had passed on all the information she had gleaned and that was enough for Alan. He was much more interested in what Pete's father was doing on Kell.

'It must be great, building roads and that,' he said. 'What exactly does he do? Does he drive one of those cranes or earth-movers or something like that, or do the measuring and mapping and such? It must be great to drive along a motorway and be able to say, "My father built this," Boy, I'd like that.'

Pete had never thought about it in that way. Because Mr Jenkins had always worked away from home, he had never seen the actual results of his work. Yet there were large areas of countryside that would be changed for hundreds of years to come, perhaps for ever, because of his father. Not many men could say that about their jobs, not people like Uncle Sam, for instance.

He felt rather ashamed to know so little about the details of his father's employment; it was not a topic that was ever discussed at home. He tried to sound more knowledgeable than he really was, but he was quite glad when Alan said it was time for them to go if they wanted to get a good vantage point in the football ground.

As they swung out of the café in a friendly group, Pete pulled his Cardiff City scarf out of his duffle bag and tossed it nonchalantly round his neck. Meirion was wearing one, he had noticed, and all the boys sported supporter's badges. Pete had brought his scarf with him but until now had been too self-conscious to wear it on this warm July afternoon. But as they got nearer Ninian Park the thickening crowd around them was full of scarf-wearers, bobble-hat wearers, boys with badges, rosettes, even one or two little boys in the complete Cardiff City strip. Pete felt like a god among gods.

Outside the football ground the crowd eddied into rows of parallel and distinct queues, each for one of the narrow entrance doors through which they had to pass in single file. There were some at the nearer end specially for boys and old age pensioners.

'We get in cheaper, see,' said Alan. He seemed to sense the kind of things Pete wanted to know but felt embarrassed to show his ignorance about. 'It's fifteen pence each, and we're in good time so we should be able to get a good place down by the wall round the ground. Of course, if you go in the stands where the seats are it's a lot dearer. I went once, when my dad took me, first time; little kids are not meant to go in the open stands – too dangerous, if there's a big crowd.'

'How dangerous?' Pete suddenly remembered his dream about the collapsing crash barrier, and, underlying it, some half-remembered news item from the past.

'Not really, not here in Cardiff. In a big match, when the stands are full it gets quite tough, with everyone cheering and swaying and pressing in on you, but that's what makes it exciting. If you're a gang of boys together you're all right. But you do get the occasional trouble-makers here, same as at any football match.'

His eyes rested speculatively on the people behind Pete, and Pete moved so that he could see who they were. There were five of them, all rather alike at first glance, close-cropped and lizard-eyed. They took absolutely no notice of Pete and the other boys, but lounged, hands in pockets, eyes flicking over the other groups of youths or the occasional boy with his long-haired girl.

'You don't want to mix with that lot,' said Alan. 'They won't bother with us though.'

The other boys were talking about Alan Perry, Cardiff's latest signing.

'Do you remember how the crowd shouted for him, that match against Sheffield Wednesday? He'd only just come to Cardiff then,' said Bill.

'I'll give him five years,' said Alan, only half joking, 'then, when the crowd shout "Alan!" it won't be for him.'

'Big-head,' said Glyn, but he did not sound very convinced.

'*Five* years?' said Meirion. 'What do you want to make it that long for? Lots of footballers make it at eighteen.' He was mocking him, but Alan answered seriously.

'That's the hefty chaps. I need that extra year to grow a bit. I can't start as young as they do, not in the professional class.'

'You could start the first team of professional midgets,' said Glyn sarcastically, but Alan was unmoved. He turned to pay at the gate, which they had now reached. Glyn said to Pete, 'He's not joking, you know. Boy, he's fast!'

'And his footwork's fab!' said Meirion. There was no doubt that, however much they might make fun of him, the other boys were disposed to accept Alan's own estimate of himself.

As Pete came up to the gate he put his hand in his pocket to get out his money. There were notices on the wall – 'Beware of Pickpockets' – and he wished he had packed some of his money at the bottom of his duffle bag instead of having it all in his pocket. He turned away from Alan and his friends to bring out the wad of notes without attracting their attention, because they would think it odd that he should have so much money on him, and as he stuffed the rest back he glanced around to see if anyone else had noticed. The skinheads they had seen earlier were in the queue right alongside him, but fortunately they seemed absorbed in their own affairs.

Then he was through the turnstile and surging across the outer yard. They climbed some steps and there they were, with surprising suddenness, at the top of the stands inside the ground. With mounting excitement Pete stared around at the great rectangle of grass in front of him and the serried ranks of seats rising around it, the standing space already filling up from the front.

'Come on,' said Alan. 'There's still some room at the barrier.' He wove his way expertly among the crowd and soon Pete found himself squeezed in among scores of eager thrusting boys right against the wall separating them from the pitch.

It was a long wait before the match was due to begin, and Pete was glad he had such good company. He would have been impatient on his own, but Alan was so entertaining, and knew so much about the private lives of all the players, that he enjoyed every minute of it. And when at last the teams ran out on to the ground, and everybody around him was yelling and cheering, he though he would burst with excitement.

At half-time, Cardiff were three-one down, which was disappointing in a way, but left hope for an exciting second-half.

'It's their defence that's weak,' said Glyn. 'Not together at all.'

'They ought to be attacking more,' said Meirion. 'They'll never get a goal if they let the ball stay in their own half all the time.'

'It's that fellow Kocik,' said Pete. 'He's too good for Jones.'

'Hey, that's right,' said Alan warmly. 'He's a smashing player.' Pete glowed at his approval.

In the second half Zodiak scored again almost immediately, and the boys fell into anxious silence; but then Cardiff suddenly got two goals in quick succession, and ten minutes later came the equalizer. Now the great stadium was pulsing with excitement, and Pete leant so earnestly over the barrier he would have fallen on to the ground, were it not for the pressure of equally excited boys behind him. And then, in the last minute, as they chanted 'Cardiff, Cardiff' with waning hopes, the Cardiff players suddenly pulled off a series of brilliant passes in mid-field, and the ball was in the net.

Up went the blue-and-white scarves swaying, outstretched, above the boys' heads and the cheering was deafening. Then the referee's whistle blew, and Alan led them over the wall in a second and out, running, running, all over the field like colts released from their stable.

As the group eventually drifted off towards the exit, Pete thought, 'If nothing else goes right for the rest of the fortnight, it will still be worth it, just for this.'

Chapter 6

PETE was sorry to part from his friends, but they were not going back into the centre of Cardiff. They all lived out at Pendinas and could get a bus straight there.

Pete walked with them towards the Pendinas road, leaving the main crowd behind. He was not in any hurry because he had two hours before his train was due to leave, so he waited at the bus-stop with the boys. Alan explained how he could cut through the back streets to get to the station.

'I'm coming to stay with Tom at the end of August,' he remarked. 'Will you be home again by then?'

'Oh, yes,' said Pete. 'I'm only going to Scotland for a fortnight.' Certainly not more, he thought; maybe a lot less. Maybe his father would put him straight on the next train home. If the other boys had not been with them, Pete would have been tempted to tell Alan the whole story, but he reflected that it would all be out in the open when Alan came in August. A disturbing thought, which he hastily put from his mind.

'I'm hoping to go on a motor-boat cruise before then,' said Alan. 'The man my sister's married, he's got pots of money and does a lot of yachting and that. Lots of people do at Pendinas. There's a yacht club he belongs to. He and my sister are going off with some friends somewhere round the coast next week and they said they'll take me with them. Should be great.'

'Hey,' said Meirion, 'here's our bus.' They all shouted goodbye and climbed aboard, standing on the step to wave as the bus bore them away.

Most of the crowd had drifted the other way from the football ground, and in any case the boys had been among the last to leave; it seemed strangely quiet after they had gone. Pete paused at the entrance to the side street, and glanced back to get his bearings. As he did so, he heard a voice say, 'Hey, there he is. I'm dead sure that's the one,' and there, a little way up the road, were the same tough-looking youths he had seen in the queue for the football ground. What was more, they were looking at him, looking with the same callous but purposeful air with which a cat watches a wounded mouse trying to escape, unhurried, but sure.

Pete turned quickly down the street. He would not let himself run, but his hands were clammy and his heart began to pound.

'Don't be stupid,' he told himself. 'This is a town; there are lots of people about.' But there were not. There was an old man, mumbling to himself and seeing nothing, and two young women who walked quickly past Pete and out into the main street he had just left.

Alan had said keep straight on at the next fork, but Pete thought if he turned left he might be able to cut back on to the main street and get in among the crowds. If the skinheads went straight on he would know they were just on their way home, and he was getting into a fuss about nothing.

But he knew, he knew, they would turn left after him, and they did.

They did not, however, follow him, but just stood at the corner, watching. When he looked round again, two of them disappeared. Then his street began to curve sharply round to the right, and he lost sight of them. The panic beating of his heart subsided a little when he realized he was alone, but he wished there was another turn to the left, because he saw that on its present course this road would not lead him back to the main street. And then he saw the two missing skinheads walking slowly up the middle of the road ahead of him. The truth dawned. This street, shut in by a curving embankment, was a crescent, both ends opening on to the road he had just left.

What should he do? If he turned round now, at sight of the two youths in front, he would be admitting to them, and to himself, that he was running away from them; that would make something come true that he still tried to persuade himself was not true. And, if it *was* true, the way behind him was barred, too.

Although his legs felt like jelly, he walked slowly onwards, but veering across to the other side of the road so that he would have a longer view around the corner behind him; then he wished he hadn't, because there were the other three spaced out across the width of the street. They began to stamp rhythmically with their heavy boots when they saw him looking.

When Pete knew for certain that he was trapped, the panic suddenly ebbed away, and he felt cool, even brave. He was still very frightened, but at least he need not pretend any more.

'They wouldn't be so stupid as to kill me,' he said to himself, 'and they're not going to rob me if I can help it.'

He marched firmly forwards, because there were three of them behind, but only two in front.

'You don't come this way, kid,' said one of them.

'Why not?' said Pete. He glanced behind and saw that the other three were closing up. He made as if to walk straight between the two ahead. That brought them together in the centre of the road. They were lumpy youths, and Pete was lithe and quick on his feet. He made a feint as though to cut through on the left, then dodged to the right. The youth put out a strong hand and grabbed him by the shoulder of his sweater. They both came down in the road together, but quick as a flash Pete bit him, hard, on the hand. Then he rolled clear and was on his feet again in an instant. The second man caught hold of his duffle bag which almost brought him down again, but he ducked and slipped it off his arm, and tore off down the road.

Whooping, the men gave chase. If Pete had known the maze of back streets as well as they did, he would have got away easily enough, but he did not. When he came out on the other street, he turned left, then right, then, facing a cul-de-sac, right again. There, ahead of him, were the gang, looking around for him. Again they split, some coming after him, some disappearing, and Pete had no idea where they would reappear. He almost collided with them at the next junction and as he sped on, one was immediately behind him. Another came loping up alongside and, instead of grabbing him, kept like that, pressing him ever closer into the wall.

Pete had never felt so frightened in his life. If they had tackled him and brought him down, at least it would have been over and done with, but this running, endless running with bursting chest and cracking muscles, and no hope of escape, this was worse than any nightmare. When at last, pressed upon mercilessly by the tormentor at his side, he blundered into the brick wall, he made no effort to regain his balance, but slid down on to the pavement against the foot of the wall, hiding his face in his hands.

He felt hot breath and heavy boots all around him, and rough hands plunging in his pockets. He knew his money was gone, but was past caring.

'Don't kill me, don't kill me,' he heard himself whimpering, and then felt a sharp blow in the ribs that made him cry out.

'Lay off it,' somebody said. 'He's only a kid. It's his money we're after, that's all.'

'I owe him something for that bite he gave me, kid or no kid,' came a surly reply, but then another voice spoke urgently.

'Look out! There's a train coming!' Hobnailed boots upon the roadway faded into silence and Pete dimly heard the churring of a diesel engine go by quite close at hand. He wondered where on earth he could have got to, but he was too wretched even to roll over and open his eyes. Then he felt a hand upon his shoulder.

He flinched and opened his eyes wide in fear.

His first impression was simply of hair – long, blond hair, and whiskers, and moustache, and flowing beard, like pictures of God. Perhaps he was dead, and it *was* God. He felt a fleeting surprise that God should look so like old-fashioned portraits of himself. Then he thought, 'But I don't want to be dead.' But at least it wasn't a face to be afraid of.

'Man,' said the face, 'that was scary.'

It dawned on Pete that the face belonged to a normal human being, a gentle rescuer. He was not dead, he wasn't even maimed for life, the nightmare was over. In his relief, helpless tears streamed down his cheeks.

The hairy vision looked at him with concern. 'Della will help,' it said. 'Come on; I don't think those blokes will come back, but they might.'

'Oh, quick,' said Pete, struggling fearfully to his feet. The vision helped him up with a pair of surprisingly brawny arms, and led him along past an old tin shed, to a creaking gate cut out of a corrugated iron fence. All the time Pete was drawing his breath in gasping uncontrollable sobs; he felt ashamed of himself, but there was nothing he could do about it; they just kept coming.

His rescuer hauled him through the gate, and lowered him gently on to a pile of old railway sleepers just inside the fence. 'You can stop here a while, if you want to,' he said, and sat down companionably beside him, gazing into space as though he had all the time in the world.

After they had sat there for a while – Pete could not tell how long – the whirling horizon began to settle and focus, and he saw they were in a kind of low ditch between the fence and an immensity of railway-lines. Most of them looked rusty and disused and splayed out from one another only to lose themselves in a wilderness of dusty grass and weeds, but a few ran gleaming and purposeful through the maze. Anyone in a train passing along the nearest of these lines would have a clear view over the fence into the street beyond. Pete wondered, with a shiver, what would have happened to him if a train had not passed when it did.

Various tin shacks and abandoned wagons stood among the sidings, and pieces of old iron and all kinds of scrap lay strewn everywhere. It was a desolate scene, but the bearded man beside him sat looking at it contentedly enough. Pete became aware of pains everywhere, especially around his ribs, and of a creeping coldness. He longed to be lying down somewhere, warm and secure, and began to be surprised at his companion for doing nothing for so long. He could see his feet, bare in tattered plimsolls, and his eyes moved up over a pair of faded jeans to a blue sweater torn at the shoulder and with bare skin showing through the rent. Was he a tramp? a hippie? a dropout? Nobody could have been more unlike Alan, yet when he spoke, he had the same directness, no pose, nothing hidden.

'Come on,' he said, 'let's go and find Della.' He led the way over the tangle of tracks.

'Who's Della?' asked Pete. He still found it absurdly difficult not to cry.

'She's my girl,' said the man, simply. 'We live over there.' There did not seem to be anywhere *to* live, just miles of sidings, and Pete steeled himself for a long trek over to the other side, and back, presumably, to civilization. But quite unexpectedly, the man swung up on to the step of an old guard's van, and opened the door.

'It's a bit high,' he said. 'Give us your hand.' He pulled Pete up after him, and closed the door. Then he walked along the corridor and into what had once been the luggage compartment. Pete, coming behind, looked through the wire partition, and saw it had been furnished, after a fashion, as a room, and part of the opposite side had been cut away to allow the light to come flooding in. A bed, made up on a large mattress laid upon the floor, took up most of the space. A young woman sat on it, holding out her arms to a staggering plump baby, coaxing him to walk the two steps to her. She must have heard them coming, because she spoke without looking up.

'Mark,' she said, 'he can walk. Look!' The baby gurgled and sat down. Mark bent and dropped a kiss on his head and went and sat beside the girl.

'Clever Thursday!' he said. 'Come on in and sit down. I don't know your name,' he said to Pete.

'Pete,' said Pete. 'Peter Jenkins.' He looked around for something to sit on, and Mark got up again.

'You'll see we haven't much proper furniture,' he said. 'We don't go much for chairs.' He gathered up several cushions and piled them in a sort of throne against the wall.

'What's the matter with him, Mark?' asked the young woman. As she looked at Pete she reminded him exactly of a Jersey calf, with enormous gentle dark eyes in a face the colour of ripe wheat. Her manner was like that too, softly inquisitive and anxious to be friends, but nervous about making the first move. Pete knew a farmer who kept Jersey cattle. Mr Thomas's Hereford calves had a blundering plunging movement when they played, or were scared, but Jerseys were altogether more delicate in their actions.

Mark told her all about the fight, and Pete realized that he must have been where he could see it happening all the time.

'Why didn't you . . .?' he began, then broke off in some confusion.

'I'm not the fighting type, friend,' Mark said. 'It wouldn't have helped, you know,' he added. 'But I expect you like heroes; I did when I was your age.'

Della got up and came over to Pete, which saved him the embarrassment of answering. She inspected his bruised face timidly, and asked if he would mind taking off his shirt so that she could see where he had been kicked. 'Put the kettle on, Mark,' she said. 'I'll make some tea.'

Mark swung the baby on to his shoulder and went along to the guard's compartment, and Della felt Pete's bruised ribs with cool careful fingers. Having diagnosed no broken bones, she fetched some water and bathed his various grazes, gained partly when he fell escaping the first time and partly when he was bulldozed into the wall.

'When you've had a cup of tea, Mark will take you home,' she said. 'Will they be worrying about you yet?'

'No,' said Pete. 'You see, I don't live near here.'

In a rather muddled manner, he told them the whole story. They did not seem particularly curious, but having started, he had to make sense of it, and even if he had not felt too tired to thread his way between what should be said and what left unsaid, it seemed unthinkable to tell calculating lies to these people.

'I don't think he should go on that train to Scotland to-night,' said Della. Pete realized she spoke with a slight foreign accent. 'He has been frightened and he needs to rest.'

'I can't anyway,' said Pete. 'I've lost my money, and my bag, and everything. What can I do?'

'That's no problem,' said Mark. 'There's enough cushions there to make a comfortable bed, and I expect we've got a spare blanket, haven't we, Della?'

'Of course,' said Della. 'Now it is July we don't need so much.'

'Have we got any food?'

'Enough,' she said. 'Tomorrow, I think it is best if you look after Thursday and I work.'

'Thursday's asleep,' said Mark, and so he was. He had crawled on to the bed and been bouncing up and down between his parents until a few moments before, but now, suddenly, he was fast asleep, rosy on the shabby pillow.

'He is beautiful,' said Della. 'Particularly when he is asleep.'

All the walls of the van were covered with paintings, mainly of railway-lines and old sheds and trucks, but in strange arrangements, their different parts jumbled up, and with all kinds of unexpected colours slotted in. 'If you painted Thursday instead of railway trains,' said Della, 'I'm sure you would be a rich man. All the world would buy pictures of Thursday to hang on their walls.'

'Thursday,' said his father, 'shall we sell you to the bourgeoisie so that we can buy you tricycles and giant teddy bears?' Thursday slept peacefully on. 'There is no point painting something so beautiful that art can only come second-best,' he went on. 'What is there to eat, Della?'

Pete, his wounds bathed and his dangers behind him, was coming over as sleepy as Thursday, propped among his cushions, but when Della produced some sort of rice dish and apples and milkless tea, because by that time they had run out of milk, he found he was quite glad to eat.

Della pulled out an extra blanket from underneath the mattress.

'Do you think you will sleep all right in the guard's compartment?' she said. 'It is rather dark in there, because there is only a small window, and of course we have no lights, but I think you are tired.'

Pete glanced up at the ceiling. Of course, there would be no power for the electric light which still stuck uselessly on the roof. It was beginning to get dusky in the cabin, and outside the random trucks were silhouetted against a deepening pink sky.

'Why can't he sleep where he is?' asked Mark. 'There's room for him.'

'Oh, Mark,' said Della, in her quaint accent, 'Peter is a big boy. He does not want to sleep with you and me and the baby.' Pete quite agreed with that, and started to get up hastily before Mark argued the matter, but Mark was not one to argue. He just smiled, and gathered the old blanket over his arm. Pete helped him to carry the cushions, wincing a little at the unexpected pain after sitting still, and Della produced a pile of old newspapers, which she spread out in a thick layer on one side of the guard's van. 'These will be softer than the boards, and they will keep you warm,' she said.

Considering that a collection of lumpy cushions on a mattress of newspapers does not make the most comfortable bed, Pete slept pretty well, though whenever a particularly noisy express hurtling by roused him he was conscious of a good many aches and pains and twice he woke from a nightmare of pursuit. Each time, as he lay awake staring into the darkness, he was overcome with the dismal realization that the money so carefully saved by his mother and Uncle Sam and his grandparents – it was all gone, and so were his clothes packed away in the duffle bag. Some time he would have to face his mother with this, as well as the unhappy story of Bongo, but not yet, he told himself desperately, not yet. Towards morning, he fell into a deeper sleep, and did not wake up until bright day shafted through the cracks of the van on to his eyelids. He could hear, then, a gentle burble of conversation, and when he went out into the corridor and looked through the wire mesh into the luggage van, Mark was kneeling on the bed changing Thursday's nappies, and talking to him.

'Where's Della?' asked Pete.

'She's had to go to work. We're out of bread.' Pete thought he meant literal bread, but he didn't; he meant money. Actual bread was about the one thing they did have left, and Pete breakfasted with Thursday on bread and jam and apples, of which there seemed an endless supply.

'They're from a greengrocer I know. I get a job sometimes sweeping up the market, and he lets me have any unsold stuff that's not worth taking home,' said Mark. 'I think, Thursday, it's going to be a painting day. What do you think?'

Thursday stared at his father unfathomably.

'Is that what you do for a living?' asked Pete. 'Painting, I mean?' He looked round at the unframed pictures festooning the walls.

'It's my way of living, but it doesn't make a living in the sense you mean it,' said Mark. 'That's why I sweep out the market, or sometimes I get a job at a warehouse, carrying stuff, or at one of the hospitals, pushing a trolley.'

'Do you like those kind of jobs?' They sounded like the sort of work that Pete's mother was determined he would never do.

'They don't hurt a person,' said Mark. 'But I'm not very quick at them,' he added seriously. 'So many people always want a person to be hurrying. That's why Della can earn more money at odd jobs than me. If we need a little money, then I go along to the Labour Exchange, but if we're down to this' – he picked up the heel of bread – 'then Della goes.'

'What does she do?'

'Whatever comes. She can always find something, because once she's worked for a person – maybe looking after their children, or scrubbing their steps – they always ask for her back. Of course they do. She is rather a special person, isn't she?'

Pete found this sort of talk confusing; this wasn't the way most men spoke about their wives.

Then he had an idea. 'Do you think if I came to the market with you, I could get a job too?' he asked. 'I've got to earn enough to get to Scotland somehow.'

'It's worth a try,' said Mark. He scooped up Thursday and an ancient bucket. 'I've got to get some more water. If I don't do Thursday's washing before I start painting I shall forget about it, and then Della would have to do it when she came home.'

It was strange, thought Pete, as they picked their way over the railway-lines, there wasn't a man in Llanwern who wouldn't call Mark a lazy good-for-nothing, yet he was sure none of them would turn to and wash a baby's nappies for their wives.

After a short distance they came to a signal box, with a stand-pipe against the wall.

'This is where we get our water,' said Mark.

'Do they know you are living in that van?' asked Pete.

'Some of the linesmen do, of course, and the signalman

from this box. He's a good guy. But when officialdom gets to know we'll have to move on.' He shook his head sadly.

'Why don't you get a proper job and have a proper house of your own?' said Pete. Then he thought he sounded rather middle-aged and severe, so he added, 'I mean, then, you could stay in a place when you liked it, and not be pushed out of it.'

'Oh, man,' said Mark, 'security is a way of living and the word they use to describe the tightest prisons. Thursday and I had better do our washing.'

When they got back to the guard's van, Mark settled on the step with an old tin bath and did the washing. Thursday sat upon a sleeper, chucking stones about. This siding was well away from the main lines and separated from them by a wedge of waste ground, where long grass and ragwort papered over the debris from discarded rolling-stock. It did not seem a very healthy place for a child to play.

'Aren't you afraid he might get run over by a train?' asked Pete.

'No,' said Mark. 'The trains can't leave their lines and neither can Thursday. He can crawl down between them but he can't get over them. It's like a very long play-pen. He'd be much worse off in a house in a street.'

'Soon he will be able to,' said Pete.

'Then we'll move, unless someone moves us first.'

'Where to?'

'I don't know. Wherever we feel like. Della thinks we ought to take Thursday to see his grandparents, so we might go there. That's how we found this place, actually.'

'This van?'

'That's right. My father and mother live in a grand house near London so we came here to get a train there, but we hadn't got enough money for the fare, and it was evening, and raining, and we needed some place, and we could see these trucks from up the road over there, so we just came. It was dark, and nobody saw us move in. It's the moving in that's tricky; if people see you starting to live in a place where nobody has lived before, they think it's all wrong, and get you turned out. But once you've been there for a bit, they reckon you just belong.'

It was not a place where Pete would have thought of living. But lying stretched out among the ragwort in the sun, with a hand upon the smooth warm rail, and a big sky overhead, it was very pleasant. In the background, goods trains came and went, self-absorbed and undemanding. All other traffic seemed far away and they were more alone than Pete would have been in his own front garden. Mark hung out the washing on a piece of string tied between an ancient gradient sign and a tumbledown cattle truck. Thursday balanced stones on Pete's prostrate body.

'Why do you call him Thursday?' he asked.

'Ah,' said Mark. 'That represents our campaign phase. We wanted to show that man is an individual.'

'Oh?' said Pete. The excitements and cares of the last week were catching up on him, and he felt very sleepy.

'People always try and turn a person into a type – "immigrant" or "uneducated" or American or Russian or Jewish – and while you make a net big enough to catch the man you find his soul has slipped out through the mesh. We thought we'd show what an accident of birth really means, by calling our baby Thursday, which is plain to everybody doesn't mean anything about him except he was born on a Thursday.'

'But it does,' said Pete, after turning this over sleepily in his mind for a while. 'My mother wouldn't call me Thursday, nor Mr Thomas, nor the vicar, nor even old Coot, I don't think. Only someone with parents like you would be called Thursday.'

'That's right!' Mark came over, suddenly absorbed, a wet pyjama-suit in his hands. 'You mean, when Thursday goes to school his teacher will say, "Poor little thing, his parents must be the kind of people who live in railway-sidings and his father paints pictures that no one will buy so his mother has to go scrubbing floors on a Sunday for them to live." Only she won't say all that, she'll just say, "Hippies". And he'll be just as much classed as anybody else.'

'Does it matter?' asked Pete.

Mark looked as though he were turning over in his mind a whole lot of arguments and couldn't decide which one to follow. Then he smiled suddenly, and said, 'There's one good thing anyway. He has a birthday once a week, and we always feel that extra bit happier on a Thursday.' He picked up the old tin bath and emptied it into the waste ground.

'I've got a picture to paint,' he said. 'May I leave Thursday piling stones on your chest while I fetch my paints and stuff?'

'M'm,' murmured Pete.

Thursday paused, a stone in his hand, and watched his father step up into the van. In due course Mark returned, with a painting from the wall under his arm, a rag-bag of paints, and an old blackboard and easel which still had a painted notice on the top: TRAIN DEPARTURES. He pinned the picture to the board, blank side outermost, and set to work.

The process was obviously familiar and soothing to Thursday, who, as soon as he saw his father take up a paint-brush, laid his head on Pete's stomach, among the stones, and went gently to sleep. Pete brushed the chippings from his chest and was soon as oblivious to the world as Thursday.

He had been living with problems for a good while now, and his nights had been getting more restless and disturbed as each one brought his planned escapade nearer. The only really good night's sleep he had enjoyed for a long time was the previous one, spent beneath the cheerful landlady's wine-coloured quilt. And a lot had happened since then.

Pete slept on the stony ground beneath a warm July sun until hunger woke him. It was not so much his hunger as Thursday's, who rose up with a crumpled cheek printed with Pete's buttons and shouted. It was quite a good-natured shout, but it was persistent and its meaning was clear. It roused Pete from his sleep first, and then it penetrated his father's consciousness. For what seemed to Pete a surprisingly long time – long enough for him to realize that he, too, was hungry – Mark remained absorbed in his painting, but when the message did get through, he laid down his brush instantly.

'Hungry already, Thursday?' he said. Then he looked at the sun, already beginning to glint down the western lines of the sidings, though still quite high in the sky.

Pete looked at his watch, but it had stopped because he had forgotten to wind it up last night.

'What's the time?' he said.

'Somewhere between three and four, I should think,' said Mark, as though this should be accurate enough for anyone. 'We'd better all find something to eat.' He picked up Thursday and went into the van, followed by Pete. There was bread, and jam, and apples, and a tin of baby food for Thursday, and tea for Mark and Pete. They finished up every scrap of bread. It wasn't an exciting meal, but it was all right. 'Fish-and-chips tonight,' said Mark happily. Pete's mouth watered at the thought.

After that, Mark went back to his painting and Thursday to his stones. Pete wandered about, feeling, not exactly bored, but patternless. He could do with more sleep, but not at once. He would have liked to kick a football around, but there was no ball and no one to play with; he might have gone exploring, but he had no wish to wander alone around the back streets of Cardiff just yet. He pottered about the sidings, examining the various relics of old steam trains and ancient rolling-stock and eventually came and stood behind Mark, watching him paint.

It was a strange picture, unlike the others on the walls of the van. Down in the bottom left-hand corner of the paper was a small screwed-up sort of shape, a bit like a mole blindly trying to burrow into a pavement. The whole of the rest of the page was covered with bits of enormous black crow-like birds, wings and hard eyes and cruel beaks, and a claw. Pete gazed at it blankly for a bit and wandered off again.

It was while he was looking around at the other pictures inside the van, with more attention than before, that he came upon a broken triangular piece of mirror, obviously used by Della when she wanted to smarten herself up to look for a job. Picking it up, he studied his face in it. All the left side was red and grazed, from the wall, but it was his right eye that looked out from a smudge of purplish-blue. He pulled up his shirt and inspected his ribs, which were still very tender, but did not show up so much. His shoulder felt stiff, and there were a good many bruises and grazes on his legs, but that was not much worse than he had often suffered in a tough game of football. But after a game of football, the next day he was ready for anything; today he felt content enough to lie about and sleep, and do nothing, and an enormous relief welled in him, that he would not have to embark on the next stage of his journey for another few days. That is, if his unusual hosts could keep him fed that long. He could not help feeling it was a pity he had not got just fifty pence of all that money that had been stolen, just something to eke out the bread and jam with a bar of chocolate, or an ice-cream. He thought of the luxurious ice-cream he had treated himself to by Cardiff Castle – was it only yesterday morning? His mind hovered cautiously about what had happened since then, and suddenly he knew what Mark's painting was about.

He walked back to Mark and went on watching him in silence for a bit.

'Do you think it's finished?' asked Mark suddenly, wiping his brushes.

'Yeah,' said Pete, 'isn't it?' It was difficult to tell. One way, it was big black crows you were looking at; another, just blots of black.

'You must say,' said Mark. 'It's your picture.'

'It's me, isn't it? Me and them skinheads.'

'It was scary,' said Mark, as he had said before. 'We've got to deal with it somehow.'

Pete did not follow this. What did Mark mean, it was his picture? Was he proposing to give it him, and if so, what on earth was he to do with it? He could hardly imagine his mother hanging it up in the front parlour, and it was a nightmarish thing to have in his bedroom.

'Della will be home soon,' said Mark contentedly. 'She must see it first.'

Pete had been doing some calculations. 'Did you realize it was Sunday?' he said in sudden surprise.

'Why not?' asked Mark, vaguely.

'Della won't be able to buy food.' He thought of that bone-bare larder gloomily.

'You can always buy food if you know where to go,' said Mark. Then he smiled. 'I forget you're a country boy,' he added. 'Cardiff is quite a place, you know. When all else fails, there's always fish-and-chip shops, and the station buffet.'

When Della eventually arrived, she looked tired, but she had a bag of station buns and two cartons of milk and a great warm newspaper bundle smelling deliciously of fish-and-chips.

They all sat among the sidings in the golden evening and ate the kind of feast that you can only appreciate if you have been living on bread and jam and apples all day. Mark was tender and attentive, and Della smiled and let him do all the fetching and carrying while she sat quiet and fed chips and flakes of fish to Thursday in her fingers.

Mark fetched his picture and showed it to her. Pete felt embarrassed that the crumpled mole in the corner should be him; and yet it *was* him; that was just how he had felt. Della studied it in silence, then she turned seriously to Pete.

'That was bad,' she said. Pete said nothing; he played with Thursday.

'Those kind of things, you've got to get rid of them,' said Mark, with decision. He went into the van and came out with a box of matches. Then he lit the bottom corner of the painting, held it up, while the paper blackened, curled and fell away in flakes light as air that drifted down the track.

They all watched in solemn silence, and Mark twisted the corner in his hands as the flame edged diagonally upwards, to keep it alight without getting his fingers burnt, until only a fragment of white remained. Then he released it and that, too, turned into a black flake before it reached the ground.

'Gone,' he said with great satisfaction. He turned to Pete. 'Better, now?'

'But you've spent all day painting that,' said Pete. 'And now you've nothing to show for it.'

'It's Sunday,' said Mark. 'Some people spend all day going to church and have nothing to show for it, but they have joined in the sacrifice for sin. This is my way.' He stretched out and took a chelsea bun. 'And Della has worked all day and brought us fish-and-chips,' he added. 'Tomorrow, it's my turn. I'll see if I can get that job in the market.'

'Can I come too?' asked Pete.

'Wait till Tuesday,' said Della. 'You still look too much as though you've been in a fight.'

Pete felt his face cautiously. He certainly did not want to draw attention to himself.

'Let's go for a walk in the park,' said Della, so Mark swung Thursday on to his shoulders and they all picked their way across the lines to the gate in the fence where Mark had pulled Pete to safety only yesterday. They followed the streets along which he had fled in panic, but now they were merely empty and shabby. They held no terror. Had Mark really killed it, reduced it to lifeless flakes?

Chapter 7

MONDAY passed pleasantly and uneventfully. Della stayed with Thursday around the guard's van, and by afternoon Pete began to feel for the first time that this life could, after a while, become dull. He prowled farther afield among the sidings, and found a large area of scrub, mainly gorse, which housed a surprising number of wild birds. Pete had always thought of bird-watching as being a country pursuit, but here was a natural bird-sanctuary, far from marauding cats and marauding boys, where no one ever laid a hedge or ploughed up a meadow, and the pippits and warblers and finches could go about their business of breeding and rearing families undisturbed.

He went to the van and scrounged a pencil and a scrap of paper, and returned to the gorse, where he sat still and quiet, as he had planned to do that Sunday so long ago, waiting for the bird-world to come to him. He did not have to wait long; he saw goldfinches and greenfinches, and of course a chaffinch, pippits and larks innumerable, and a persistent willow-warbler softly rippling as it searched for insects on a scraggy willow sapling that had grown up through an ancient disused buffer. A wagtail swooped and bobbed among the chippings and a dunnock moved through the undergrowth as earth-bound as a mouse. Pete had scarcely become aware of a family of half-fledged blackbirds, hopefully pursuing their parents for food, when one of the adult birds flew off with a strident shriek, and the young ones froze and melted from sight. Pete wondered if he had made a movement to startle them, but then he saw a shadow, strangely motionless, on the chippings, and looking up, observed a kestrel hovering overhead. As soon as its eye was caught by Pete's upturned face, it sailed off and started to hover again a couple of hundred yards farther on, but the small bird world stayed hidden for a long spell after that.

As nothing was happening, Pete's mind turned to his own immediate future. He remembered his mother would be waiting to hear from him, from Germany. He would hate her to turn up trustingly on Friday to see the headmaster before she had received a letter from him telling her the true story. On the other hand, it would scarcely comfort her to get a letter from him now. 'Dear Mum,' he would have to say, 'I am living in a guard's van on a railway-siding with some people who have no money and do odd jobs when they feel like it. I was attacked by skinheads and had my money stolen, and my bag with all my things in. I am trying to get to Scotland to see Dad, but he doesn't know I am coming and I don't know how I am going to get there. I hope you are well. Love from Pete.'

No letter would be better than that. Considering he had now been three nights away from home, he had not got very far.

A large grasshopper landed on his hand and stayed there to groom itself, so still was he sitting. Moving his eyes carefully while keeping the rest of himself motionless, Pete glimpsed a sudden short movement on the overgrown railway-line and saw three, no four, lizards sunning themselves on the warm metal. And he could hear a soft continuous purring, as of a fishing-reel running out – could that be a grasshopper warbler? He had read about the noise in books, and his grandfather had described it to him, but they were not common birds and this was the first time he had ever heard the song, if such it could be called. Grandad would like this bird-haunted scrub, but he would be uneasy at the urban skyline, bounded by ragged spiked fences and terraced roofs and lines of goods trucks, with the huge gantry bearing the floodlights for the football ground towering up above the grandstand roof.

Pete wondered what Scotland would be like, and especially Kell, and, not for the first time, what sort of a welcome he would get from his father.

This brought him to the immediate problem of money, for without it how was he to get there? He could try and hitch-hike, but it would take some time and even if he slept rough he would not be able to manage without food. In any case, something at the pit of his stomach said No. His experience with the thugs saw to that.

There was Alan. Of course there was Alan. Why ever had he not thought about him before?

For a moment everything was suddenly all right. Alan would know what to do, and how to do it, just as he had known at the café and in the football ground. He was on the telephone, so it would be easy to find his address in the directory – no, better still, he could ring him up and explain things first, without the risk of meeting the rest of Alan's family before he had been able to tell him the whole story. He would enjoy that; he began to cast around in his mind for the phrases that would paint the bewildering events of the last few days in the colours of adventure.

For some reason Mark's picture, now destroyed, came unexpectedly into his mind, and his imagination faltered. He had not been planning to mislead Alan in any way, and yet the picture he had in mind to paint for him would have been very different from Mark's, with its uncomfortable shudder of truth. Alan would produce a plan for him, he felt sure; but maybe his plan for the future would have the same touch of make-believe as Pete's picture of the past, and it would be Pete who would have to put it into action.

Of course he would go and see Alan, but not yet, Pete decided. In any case, he had not even got the two pence for a phone call, still less the bus fare to Pendinas. Alan would not know what it was like to face the world absolutely penniless; Pete fancied that he would feel bolder about carrying out one of Alan's plans if he had got some money in his pocket.

The first thing to do was to earn some, as quickly as possible. He got up and hurried home along the railway tracks, almost as though he could catch himself a job by running after it, even now, at six o'clock in the evening.

Mark had just come home and was soaping the market dust out of his golden beard in a bucket outside the guard's van while Thursday stared at him, entranced, in the evening sunlight. Della was cooking supper inside, and a delicious smell of stew wafted out over the sidings. A little later she brought out bowls and a steaming saucepan, and they all sat among the ragwort eating stew and hunks of bread.

Pete, however, was too eager about getting a job to sit still and be peaceful. Although he knew there was nothing to be done about it that evening he was too impatient, or perhaps too rested, to be idle, and he busied himself clearing away the bowls and washing up, and trying to discover from Mark what job prospects there were.

Mark was willing enough, but vague. He had, however, got a job lined up at the market for himself tomorrow, and he thought they would agree to take on Pete as well.

'I've got to earn enough to pay my train fare to Oban,' said Pete, 'and for the boat over to Kell. How much do you suppose that will be?' Nobody knew, and Mark said he thought Pete would be lucky to earn more than fifty pence in the day. 'I don't know why, because you'd do the job better than me,' he said humbly, 'but they don't pay boys as much as men.' At least that gave Pete one job he could do straightaway. He climbed over the fence into the streets and ran along to the station, where he inquired the cost of a half-single ticket to Oban. The answer was nearly five pounds. Sobered, Pete walked back to the guard's van. At that rate, he would still be working for his fare when it was time for his father to come home.

Next morning he woke early, and set off eagerly with Mark through the quiet streets to the market. The man who employed Mark glanced at Pete and said it was all right by him if it was all right by Mark and if they got the junk cleared and the place swept they could earn themselves a couple of quid. Mark, though apparently leisurely, was strong and conscientious, and Pete, in a fever to earn himself big money, toiled away as hard as he had ever worked in his life. As a result, they had finished the job and collected the money by midday.

'Ta,' said the man. 'That was quick.' He looked at Mark. 'You come in tomorrow if you like and see if there's anything for you, but I can't promise anything for the boy.'

He strolled off and Pete looked uncertainly at Mark. 'Isn't there anything else we can do?' he asked.

'Not today,' said Mark. 'We've got it done twice as fast today, being two of us, so now we can have a half-day off.'

That wasn't at all what Pete wanted, and he realized that all he had done was taken a half-share in Mark's pay-packet. Mark, however, did not seem to mind.

'I've got enough,' he said, 'and now we can be at home for the rest of the day. I shall paint.'

Pete sighed. His conscience told him that he really owed his share to Mark anyway, for all the meals he had eaten with them since Saturday, but he had to admit that just now he needed money much more than Mark appeared to do.

As they came in sight of 'home', they were surprised to see three uniformed railway officials prowling round the van.

'What are they doing, do you think?' asked Pete, with a sudden surge of alarm.

'Their job, I expect,' said Mark, sadly. 'It looks as though we've got to the bottom of the page, and we'll have to turn over.' He walked quickly over to Della, who was sitting silently on the grass verge, Thursday in her arms, and sat down beside her. The peaked caps took absolutely no notice of any of them, but went on examining the van, inside and out, with great thoroughness.

'Do you think they'll sue us for wilful damage?' Mark asked Della. 'That window I cut out.'

'I'm glad you've come home,' was all she said.

At last the inspection was finished and the three peaked caps re-emerged. One of them bore down on Mark and Della.

How small they both look, Pete thought suddenly. And – yes, scruffy. Like a tinker family.

The official took out his notebook.

'How long have you been squatting here?'

'About six months,' said Mark.

'No, more,' said Della. 'We had a lovely Christmas here. We must have come in November.'

'I don't know how it hasn't been reported before,' said the man.

'Have we been a nuisance?' said Della.

'You're trespassing for one thing,' said the man. 'You shouldn't be here at all, let alone *living* in this van. *And* you've damaged British Rail property. Look at this.' He pointed to the hinged unglazed window through which the July sun was flooding.

'It will shut up again,' said Mark. 'We had to do that so that we could keep the rain out – well, mostly – in a storm.'

'That's not the point,' said the man. 'We could sue you for trespass and damage.'

'You can have my pictures,' said Mark. 'I haven't got anything else.'

The man looked unimpressed. 'They're good,' said Della. 'One day they'll be worth thousands of pounds, perhaps.'

'*Per*haps,' said the man.

Mark got up, smiling courteously. 'Thank you for leaving us so long,' he said. 'We've had a very happy life here, haven't we, Della?'

'What a place to bring up a child,' muttered one of the

others. 'It isn't fit. Whatever would the welfare people say?' Pete could not help smiling; it was exactly what his mother would be saying if she were here.

'When do we have to go?' asked Della.

'Right now,' said the official. 'The best thing for you to do is go along to the social services people and see if they can fix you up for a night or two, and then come back and collect your belongings. Now, I must get your particulars first. Name?'

'Mark and Della and Thursday,' said Mark. 'And Pete, but he's just staying with us.'

'Mark what?'

'Gibson.' It was the first time Pete had heard his surname.

'Address?'

Mark paused a moment. 'Guard's Van, Cardiff Central,' he said.

'I mean permanent address.'

'Man,' said Mark, 'there's nothing permanent about life.'

The man wrote 'No fixed abode' in his book. He asked a number of other questions and made some more notes in his little book. Then he closed it carefully, fastening it with a black elastic band.

'Now,' he said, quite kindly, as though he were speaking to children, 'you've got the rest of the day to find yourselves other accommodation. You go straight along to the Department of Social Security' – and he gave them the address – 'and I expect they can put you up in hostels, one for the mother and baby and one for you.' He looked at Pete. 'Has this boy got a home of his own?' he asked.

'I'm on my way to Scotland,' said Pete hastily.

'That's lucky,' said the official. 'That's one less to worry about.'

'Please,' said Della, 'don't worry about us. There's really no need to.'

'That's right,' said Mark, earnestly. 'Man, you've got a lot of responsibility – all this ...' he waved his hand vaguely around the sidings. 'You don't need to feel responsible for us.'

The man sighed. 'Some people,' he said. 'There ought to be places for people like you.'

'There are,' said Mark. 'Lots of them, if you know where to look. We'll find some place. But not hostels,' he added.

'And not railway property,' said the man. He glanced at Mark suspiciously. 'I could get the police here,' he said, 'but I won't do that. Not yet. But if you're not out of here by evening, lock, stock and barrel, I shall have to get them. Then it won't be a hostel, but a night in the cells for you, most likely.'

At last he was gone, and the other two men with him.

They all sat in silence on the step and watched them go.

'Pity,' said Mark. 'But it was bound to happen some time. It was too good to last.'

Thursday had dozed off, and Della laid him down between the sleepers. A smile twitched at the corner of his mouth but otherwise he showed no hint of the impending upheaval. Then they went in and stared through the lattice at the place that had been home to all of them.

'I suppose we shall just have to leave the mattress,' said Mark. 'And the pictures, and some of the cushions.'

Della was finding remnants of food in the cardboard box that served as a larder. 'We'd better eat what we can now,' she said. 'Let's start with the apples.'

They all went out again and settled down beside Thursday. There was a question that Pete felt needed to be asked.

'Where,' he said, 'are you going *to*?'

Mark and Della chewed in silence. 'Tell you what,' said Mark at length. 'What if Pete and I had a look around first?'

'Mark,' said Della, 'I suppose we haven't enough money to get to London tonight?' Mark shook his head. 'I was only thinking it seemed a pity having got here ready to go to your parents, to move away again.'

'I doubt it,' said Mark. 'It's not important, moving away again.'

'I'm worried,' said Della.

Mark put his hand on her knee. 'That's bad,' he said. 'You mustn't begin worrying; we never have.'

'It's what they said about Thursday,' said Della. Her eyes rested on him, lying rosy and peaceful among the chippings. 'Supposing we don't find anywhere? Supposing we're out on the streets tonight and the police pick us up? They could take Thursday. They'd say I wasn't a fit person to look after him.'

There was a long pause. Then Mark said, 'How much money have we got, then?'

'You've got a pound,' said Della. 'Let's see.' She went into the van and came out with an old shopping-bag, from which she eventually produced two pound notes, two fifty-pence pieces and seventeen pence in loose change. 'Three pounds seventeen. Four pounds seventeen with yours. Is that enough?'

'I don't know,' said Mark. He felt in his pocket and produced a few more coppers.

They sat there, bewildered and undecided, and Pete felt it was time he took charge.

'I'll go down to the station and find out,' he said. 'If you give me the money I can get your tickets if it's enough.'

'What'll you do after we've gone?' asked Della. 'If you can get the tickets.'

'I've got a friend,' said Pete. 'Lives out at Pendinas. I can go there.'

'Are you sure?'

'Yes, of course.' Pete spoke more confidently than he felt. 'I'd have gone there on Saturday if you hadn't rescued me. Anyway, I've got some money now, what I earned today.'

'If you're sure,' said Della. 'Anyway,' she added, 'that probably won't buy our tickets, in which case we'll still be around.' She turned and looked in at the open window. 'Mark, we'll need some sort of crate. Can you get one from the dump?'

They seemed to have forgotten Pete already, so he took the

four pounds and set out for the station. He left them the rest – after all, they would need *some* money for the journey.

He looked up train departure times first. There seemed to be plenty of trains going that evening so he went along to the ticket office and asked for two singles to London.

The tickets flicked out on the counter before him. 'Four ninety,' said the clerk casually. 'Next, please.'

For a moment Pete looked at the four notes clutched in his hand. Then he put his other hand in his pocket and, adding his own note to the bundle, laid them all upon the counter. 'Thank you. Four ninety – five pounds.' The ten-penny piece rattled out and Pete took it and the two tickets and left.

Well, he had done it now. He could not go back and say he had changed his mind and did not want the tickets after all. Anyway, there was Alan. And he still had tenpence.

When he got back to the guard's van Della was stowing all their household goods into a slatted crate which had the name of a banana firm stencilled on one end. Mark was inside taking down the pictures. Thursday was sitting quietly eating an apple.

'Were you able to get them?' Mark asked.

'Yes,' said Pete. 'Just.' He was embarrassed not to offer any change, but neither of them seemed to give the matter a thought.

'I think if we're going we should go as soon as we can,' said Della. She took the tickets and put them in her bag without looking at them. 'Thank you, Pete,' she said. 'That was kind of you. Mark, don't you think you should ring your people and ask if it is all right to come?'

Mark appeared in the doorway, his arms full of papers. 'Oh, I don't know. We needn't go right away, as soon as we get there. We could find some place to shack up, and go around in a few days' time and see them. Then we can play it from there.' He disappeared back inside the van.

Della stood still, her arms full of old rags and newspapers, drooping a little. Then she felt Pete's eyes resting on her, and turned to smile at him before dumping the rubbish and getting some matches out of her jeans pockets. She coaxed the flame, then, when it strengthened, sat back and watched it spread.

'Everyone's afraid of something, I suppose,' she said.

Pete did not say anything, but when Della glanced up and saw that he was listening, she went on. 'I don't know whether Mark's afraid that staying with his parents will kill our life together, or just afraid they won't like me and I'll get hurt.'

'Surely,' said Pete, surprised, 'grown-ups aren't afraid of their parents?'

Della laughed. 'It's the beard,' she said. 'But beards don't mean much. In seven years you'll be as old as Mark.'

They were soon ready to go, for there was not much to pack that was worth the trouble of taking. Pete peered into the compartment before he left and it just looked like a derelict old guard's van where someone had dumped a dirty mattress and a few old railway cushions and a stack of papers. Mark had taken down the pictures and stowed them in a corner because he needed the string they were hanging from to tie down the lid of the crate. On the back of the top painting he had scrawled, 'Rent for six months, with the compliments of the artist.'

As they went into the main station hall, Pete noticed Mark had disappeared. He had been a little way behind them, and now he was nowhere to be seen.

'Where's Mark?' he asked Della.

'I expect he is ringing his father,' she said, nodding towards the far end of the entrance. There stood their crate, outside a row of telephone booths.

'I thought he wasn't going to,' said Pete. 'Or did you persuade him after?'

'No,' said Della. 'But he was screwing himself up to do it.'

Pete still felt puzzled, but he was glad Mark had changed his mind. After all, he had made quite a sacrifice to get those tickets and if Mark, in his own words, was merely going to 'shack up somewhere' when they got to London they could just as well be doing it in Cardiff, if not better.

There was a restaurant near by, and a lovely smell of food drifted over to them. Pete realized how hungry he was. Della must have been thinking the same thing because she said hopefully, 'I wonder if Mark will have any change left from the phone call. Just a cup of tea would be nice.'

'You'll need all your change for the journey,' said Pete. Feckless, that's what Mum would say, he thought, grinning to himself. He walked out into the forecourt, just to get away from the smell of food while waiting for Mark, but he had only been there a couple of minutes when he heard a voice calling, 'Here, you, boy!'

Pete turned and saw a taxi-driver leaning out of his cab.

'Got a lady here, wants a porter,' said the driver. 'See if you can find one, there's a good lad – unless,' he added, 'you fancy the job yourself.'

'Oh, yes, please,' said Pete quickly. It seemed a busy moment at the station; several trains were due and the crowds were thickening at the ticket booths and the barrier.

'Better get yourself a platform ticket, then, if you haven't got one,' said the man, as the old lady paid him off.

That was a problem. 'I haven't any money,' said Pete.

The driver grunted a little suspiciously, but the old lady must have given him a handsome tip because he took fivepence out of it and handed it over to Pete.

'Now be sure you look after her luggage properly, mind,' he said. 'She's one of my regulars, and not so young as she was – and a bit deaf,' he added in a husky whisper. 'It's the Bristol train she wants, first class compartment.'

The old lady thanked the driver and turned to Pete. 'Are

you sure you can manage?' There were two expensive-looking small suitcases, very neat and light, and Pete nodded. 'Do you think you could get my ticket for me? I can't always hear what they say. First class to Bristol, you tell them.' Pete followed her into the station, and set down the suitcase near the barrier. He managed to murmur. 'Got a job – see you on the platform,' to Della as he joined the queue, the old lady's five-pound note in his hand, thinking how lucky he was to have collected a platform ticket as part of the job. Otherwise he would not have been able to see his friends on to their train.

The old lady seemed both trusting and easily grateful, and since she talked away without expecting any reply, about which compartment she preferred and what part of the platform to aim for, and how she liked her luggage stowed, Pete was able to look as if he knew what he was doing. As he carefully closed the carriage door after her, his eye on a genuine porter farther down the train doing the same thing, she pressed twenty pence into his hand.

As a result, Pete rejoined Mark and Della on their platform ten minutes after he had parted from them and twenty pence richer. They all celebrated on it modestly in the refreshment room; it did not go very far but Pete did not want to produce his tenpenny piece, partly because he thought he might need it but mainly because he did not want to risk bringing up the question of the tickets again.

It was only when the London train was actually in the station, and Mark and Della climbing aboard with Thursday and their ridiculous luggage, that alarm began to stir deeply in Pete's stomach. To be money-less and homeless in their company had seemed unimportant, but now the shadow of loneliness fell suddenly upon him.

Mark disappeared into the train, busy settling the crate and Thursday, but Della turned and smiled down on Pete, a forlorn figure on the crowded platform.

'Then it's good-bye,' she said.

'Good-bye,' said Pete.

'You'll be all right?' she said. 'You've got your money from the market safe, haven't you?'

Pete nodded. What there was left of it was safe enough.

'I'll be fine,' he said. 'I can look after myself, even if I haven't got a beard.' They both laughed. 'Is it all right about Mark's family?' Pete added. 'You are going there tonight?'

'Yes,' said Della. She sighed.

'I thought you wanted that,' said Pete.

'Yes,' said Della. 'I did, because I was afraid for Thursday. But now also I am a little afraid for Mark and me, just like Mark was.'

'Why?'

'I think rich people, successful people, can be rather frightening, don't you? Especially if they are kind. They want to give you things you don't want to have. I think Thursday's grandmother will give him a beautiful cot, and lovely toys, and new clothes, and Thursday will cry for green apples and railway-lines; and maybe it will be a bit the same for us.' She gazed out over the busy platform, a pool of sunlight in the dark station. 'I would like us to be going with you to Kell.'

'If I ever get there,' said Pete.

'Of course you will. And we will get to our place one day.'

'Where's that?'

'I don't know. Some place where we can live and be ourselves.'

'Like the guard's van?'

'I expect so.'

Doors were shutting and people beginning to wave good-bye.

'I liked it in the guard's van,' said Pete.

'I'm glad,' said Della. 'It was a happy place. I hope you find your Kell, and we find ours.'

'Yes,' said Pete. 'I hope you do.'

'I think we will,' said Della. 'In one form or other. If we keep waiting patiently and remember how to be ourselves.'

The train slid quietly away. Mark appeared behind Della, Thursday under one arm, and then all three were carried away out of sight.

Chapter 8

PETE turned and walked quickly towards the way out, feeling that unless he contacted Alan immediately he was going to get panicky. However, when he saw an elderly man in front of him standing by a large suitcase and trying to attract the attention of a porter, he ran up to him. Portering could be a profitable business, he had discovered.

'Can I take your case, sir?' he asked, feeling an old hand by now.

But before the old gentleman had time to answer, Pete was shouldered roughly aside by the tall young porter he had seen by the train earlier.

'You're not employed on this station to my certain knowledge,' said the youth, 'so you can go and get yourself a job some place else. Where are you travelling to, sir?' He picked up the heavy suitcase and slung it on to his trolley. 'I've been watching you,' he added to Pete, 'and my advice to you is scarper, quick sharp.'

Pete scarpered. The porter did not look vicious, like the skinheads, but he certainly wasn't friendly, and Pete was taking no chances.

He gave up his platform ticket at the barrier, changed his tenpence into coppers at the newspaper stand, and made straight for the telephone booths. Finding one empty, he closed the door carefully behind him and took out the big local directory. There appeared to be a formidable number of Protheroes living in the Cardiff area, but eventually he found the one he wanted: H. Protheroe, Ael-y-bryn, Elm Road Pendinas. After reading the instructions several times over, Pete picked up the receiver and dialled the number. As he listened anxiously to the ringing tone he tried to make up his mind what he was going to say if the phone was answered by some unknown relation of Alan's.

Luck was with him. The ringing stopped abruptly as the receiver at the other end was lifted, and a familiar confident voice said, 'Pendinas 3584.'

'Alan?' said Pete. He suddenly felt confused and shy, and realized he had not thought out the conversation at all beyond this point. 'It's Pete,' he said.

'Pete?' said Alan's voice, obviously puzzled.

'Peter Jenkins. I came to the football match with you; do you remember?'

During the pause Pete had time to wonder whether he would remember, and if he did, would be at all interested in him now, or in the least inclined to help him, but when Alan spoke again it was reassuring.

'Pete? Have you got to Kell?' At least he had not forgotten about his affairs, but Pete felt a little foolish at having to tell him he was ringing from Cardiff station.

'Cardiff? I thought you were going to Scotland that evening?'

'I was, but all sorts of things have happened since then – I was robbed of all my money . . .'

'Robbed?'

'Yeah, those skinheads, do you remember them at the football match?'

'You're joking!'

'No, honest. Do you remember them?'

'Yes, of course I do; go on, then. This is fab!'

It was an encouraging reaction. Pete grew more fluent in his story, and soon brought it up to date. Alan was flatteringly enthralled and distinctly envious.

'Gosh, that's great!' he said. 'But why didn't you get on to Auntie Bron to let your Mum know what had happened?'

Pete realized how much Alan still didn't know.

'Look,' he said, 'I've got an awful lot to tell you, only I don't know how long this call will go on for, and you mustn't let your people know about me. Can I meet you somewhere?'

'You bet!' said Alan. 'I'm bored stiff this afternoon. My mum's around making jam, and you haven't got any money anyway, so I'll come in to Cardiff, and meet you outside Ninian Park, the main entrance, you know.'

'Can you do that?' began Pete, but just then the time limit expired and they were cut off. Trust Alan, he thought, to get everything organized in ten seconds flat.

It took him about a quarter of an hour to get to Ninian Park. By now he was fairly familiar with the general layout of the area, and the floodlighting gantries were visible from a good many vantage points. He had looked out over one of them every day from the guard's van.

As he rounded the last corner and came within sight of the main entrances where he had queued so expectantly a few days earlier, he saw Alan leaning against the wall, perched on the saddle of a smart yellow bicycle.

'You've been quick,' said Pete. 'How far away do you live then?'

'Four miles, but it's all downhill,' said Alan. 'And I fairly speeded.'

Pete felt gratified that Alan should be so impatient to hear the rest of his story. There was a park immediately across the road, to which Alan nodded.

'We'll go and sit in there,' he said. 'Come on.' As soon as they found an empty bench they sat down and Alan turned to Pete eagerly.

'Let's have it, then,' he said. 'Why is it all a secret, and – gosh, where'd you get that black eye? Come on, come on, out with it.'

Filling in the adventures between now and the football match was easy; and it all came out as Pete had imagined that day among the gorse bushes. But going back before that was a great deal more difficult. When he had told his story to Mark and Della he had been too tired to worry much about the impression his part in the tobacconist's raid might make on them, and had not said more about it than was necessary to explain his present predicament, nor had they asked any questions; but Pete sensed that Alan would be a more acute and critical audience.

As he floundered through the chain of events that had led him to run away from home, working backwards reluctantly in response to Alan's relevant queries, he became aware that after a while the questioning died away and Alan was listening in grave silence.

The pauses grew longer between each sentence as Pete let his mind wander back uncomfortably over those last unheroic weeks, and with each pause Pete felt himself dwindle from the cool and generous person who had arranged Mark and Della's shattered lives for them to the shabby and shame-faced schoolboy flipping a stolen fag into the river, those long weeks ago in Aberafon.

Alan had still said nothing, but sat withdrawn and serious, splitting a blade of grass with slim dark fingers.

Pete looked at him morosely, wishing he would speak. Urged on by a sort of death-wish, he continued, as though inviting Alan's condemnation, 'Tom was proper fed-up with me. With him feeling like that, I suppose going to Germany would have been a mess-up anyway.'

Alan threw away the grass with an air of finality. 'Damn, I wish I was you,' he said.

Pete stared at him. 'Me?' he asked.

'Yeah,' said Alan. 'You're like a grown-up; you do things for real. Me, I just live like a boy, waiting for the future.'

'But that's not true,' exclaimed Pete, genuinely astonished.

'I'm just the opposite. You can always organize things so that they go right, but I just muddle and am afraid to speak my mind – haven't got a mind, I suppose – and if I was like you say, then I wouldn't have made such a mess of things.'

'What mess, then?' asked Alan. 'Look at all the adventures you've been having, much more exciting than parading around Germany with a lot of school kids, and the way you've planned it out and everything – and look at those skinheads; I mean I bet it was frightening and that, but it was a proper real-life thing to happen, not just kicking a ball around the back garden while your mother makes jam, which is all I was doing when you rang up.'

Pete shook his head wonderingly. He supposed that what Alan said about his adventures being real-life was true, and yet he didn't feel a bit like that. Was it only the adventures that happened to somebody else that seemed real?

'You wouldn't have got caught up in all that stealing business,' said Pete with conviction. 'If you had, you'd have known what to do, and not just been too scared to say anything to Steve and them.' It was strange how, in talking to Alan, he found himself able, for the first time, to put his finger on the place that hurt. 'I was mad with the headmaster because he just took it for granted I was a thief, and I was mad with Tom and them who thought I'd been double-dealing on purpose, but really I should be mad with myself for being such a coward.'

'It wouldn't have happened to me, because the boys wouldn't have let me in on it, because I'm too bossy,' said Alan, disarmingly. 'They like me around to think up schemes for them, but if they've got a scheme of their own then I'm out.' He laughed. 'So come on, I want to see where everything happened, and the guard's van and everything.' He got up.

Pete did not stir, but sitting on the bench in the sunshine, looking up into Alan's open face, he knew he had not felt so unlonely since the days before he and Tom had quarrelled. It was nice to remember he had made it up with Tom after a fashion, and Alan was Tom's cousin and coming to stay with him. But a lot had got to be seen to before then.

'Hey, wait a bit,' he said. 'You can think up a scheme for me then, to get to Kell when I've only eightpence in my pocket and no clothes but these.'

'Oh, I'll think of something,' said Alan nonchalantly. 'We'll make a plan as we go.' He stood with his hand resting on the centre of the handlebars of his bike, ready to go, so Pete stood up, too, rather reluctantly, and they began to stroll back and along the road to the bus-stop where Alan and his friends had left him after the match. Alan insisted that he wanted to retrace every step from there to the guard's van. Pete led him confidently along as far as the crescent where he had first been ambushed, but soon got confused when he tried to follow the route of his twisting flight, and was even unsure about the actual spot where he had been brought to the ground and robbed. Now, in company and at peace there seemed nothing to differentiate one piece of brick-walled alley from another, and it was only after climbing through the bent gate in the corrugated iron fence and getting his bearings in the more familiar railway-sidings that he could definitely place where it had all happened.

While he was dithering about, trying to make sure, Alan was examining the whole area with interest, and suddenly he gave a shout. He had leant his bicycle against the fence and was standing on the saddle to see over the top into the derelict sidings.

'Hey!' he said. 'There's a duffle bag along there.' He had his chin on the top of the fence and was peering sideways along the nettle-grown ditch on the other side. 'Could it be yours?'

'Where?'

'About fifty yards along there.' Alan scrambled down off his bike and leaving it there, squeezed through the gate and disappeared. Pete followed and caught him up as he stooped and picked up his find.

There was no doubt that it was Pete's bag. They emptied it out on the ground, pyjamas, socks, toothbrush, thick jersey, anorak, everything that Pete had carefully stuffed into it before he left.

'To think it must have been here all the time!' said Pete. It was less than two hundred yards from where he had been living.

'I expect they didn't want to be caught with it in case you reported the attack to the police and it would give the show away, so they just chucked it over the fence,' said Alan. 'I suppose none of your money was in it?'

'No,' said Pete. 'They got that out of my pockets when they pulled me down, but they grabbed the bag earlier, by mistake really, when they were trying to catch me.' He looked at his belongings, scattered among the stunted docks, and felt an unexpected wave of homesickness. His mother had sat knitting that jersey ready for him to take to Germany, now and again breaking into his homework or interrupting his view of the television to measure the length against him.

'I must write to Mum so as she knows what's happened before she goes to see the Head on Friday,' he said.

'It'll be easier now you've got your clothes back,' said Alan.

'Yeah,' said Pete. Alan was right. His mother would have minded more about the clothes than about the money, so long as he was all right. But was he all right? A renewed sense of desperation welled up in him, partly set off by the sight of the familiar home clothes, partly by hunger, and he glanced at his watch, realizing the day was slipping by and he was still homeless and almost penniless. Alan was a good companion, but he hadn't actually solved any problems for him.

'It's all very well for you,' he said, a trifle crossly. 'When you've finished enjoying my adventure you can go home and have supper, but what am I supposed to do?'

Alan began to stuff Pete's belongings back in his bag while Pete watched him disconsolately. Finding the bag should have cheered him up, but in fact it had done the opposite.

'There's two things you can do,' said Alan. 'Either you can come home with me and we can explain the whole story, or as much as we have to, to my parents, and you can have supper and stay the night with us, and I suppose Dad will insist on getting on to them up at Tygwyn and so to your mum, and probably take you home tomorrow by car, or . . .'

'Yes?' said Pete.

'Or, I can hide you in the garden shed or somewhere, and smuggle you food, and try and find you a job until you earn enough money to get to Kell – if you still want to go there, that is.'

Did he still want to go there? Pete had never questioned it and nothing had happened to make his return home any less painful, but now he hesitated, for the first time.

He shook his head gloomily. 'I don't know,' he said. Alan's plan had shown him a convenient escape route, if going back home penniless and before the storm broke could be called an escape. Hitherto, to get home had demanded as much initiative as to go on to Kell, but now, if he gave in, everything would be arranged, whereas if he held out – well, Alan's plan for that decision sounded distinctly incomplete.

Alan had been watching his face. There was no doubt which way he wanted Pete to decide, but he was not unsympathetic.

'Look,' he said. 'Don't make up your mind now. Come and show me the guard's van, and then I've got enough money to get some chips.'

'That's the best suggestion you've made yet,' said Pete. 'I'm starved.'

He led the way over the lines, keeping a wary eye out for officials, but the place seemed as deserted as it had been the first time Pete came there. When they reached the guard's van it looked just as Pete had last seen it, shabby and empty and lifeless.

'And a family really lived here all those months?' exclaimed Alan. Even for Pete it seemed hard to believe how homely it had been only a few hours ago. He tried to describe how it had looked, and to explain to Alan something of the atmosphere of the place. His friend looked about him, eager to meet him half-way but clearly finding it difficult.

'What are all these papers?' he asked. 'Why, they're paintings!' While Pete told him about Mark's painting, and about the one he had destroyed, Alan turned them over one by one, fascinated.

'I'm sure they're good!' he exclaimed. 'I know they look like nonsense, some of them, but they're just like the things they put in exhibitions of modern art in the National Museum of Wales, and places like that. Did he ever sell any of them?'

'Not that I know of,' said Pete. 'I don't think he tried, much. He just liked painting.'

'Well, I'm going to try,' said Alan, busy sorting them out into tidy bundles. 'If he doesn't want the money, you do.'

'He did put on the top about them being rent for the van,' said Pete dubiously.

'Don't be daft,' said Alan. 'However you got mixed up in a burglary beats me, you're so law-abiding. You know he didn't expect them to take it like that, and I'll bet they don't either. They'll just chuck the lot on the nearest rubbish dump.' Remembering all the stuff on the dump farther up the sidings, Pete was inclined to agree. He hated to think of all those pictures lying rotting among the weeds up there.

'Anyway,' Alan went on, 'we can leave them the top one – that's the one he wrote on, after all, so he didn't need to have meant all of them, did he? And they can have that one, it's dirty, and this one, that's too big to fit in with the others, and this one, that I don't think much of.' He was happily re-sorting them when a dark shadow fell across the doorway. Both boys swung round quickly. It was the railway official again.

'You still here?' he said to Pete. 'Where have the others gone?'

'Taken the train to London,' said Pete.

'And what about you? And what's this other boy doing here?'

Pete did not know what to say, but Alan was unflappable. 'We're off to Scotland in a day or two,' he said. 'I'm just helping him clear up.' He waved at the pictures. 'The artist who lived here said some of these were for the rent for the guard's van, and we were trying to sort out which ones you might like.' He pointed to the message scrawled on the top one. It did not help to make the picture look like a valuable work of art.

'Well, you can take the lot as far as I'm concerned,' remarked the man. 'We're a railway company, not an art dealer.'

'May we really?' said Alan, naïvely. 'We'd better leave you that one, just to please the artist, but if you'd like us to clear away the others we'll do that.'

'You can do what you like,' said the man, 'only get out, quick sharp.'

'Oh, thanks,' said Alan. 'Come on, Pete, you take that bundle and I'll take all these. Cheerio.' He marched off down the line, his arms full of paintings, followed with less assurance by Pete.

'See? It's easy,' he remarked. 'All you need is a bit of cheek.'

'What are we going to do with them now?' asked Pete.

'I know a shop where they sell all sorts of peculiar arty things,' said Alan. 'In one of the arcades, it is. Rather a long way from here, though. Do you think you can manage without dying of hunger?'

Pete was doubtful, but it is difficult to buy or eat chips when carrying armfuls of valuable unframed paintings, so they decided to stick it out.

In the event, Pete was glad they had. The owner of the shop – a pale, bony middle-aged man with the long hair of a teenager – turned over the pictures dubiously, talking a lot about the poor market and the cost of mounting and framing, asked a few questions to make sure the boys had come by the paintings honestly, and then, just when Pete thought he was going to turn them away, said grudgingly, 'I'll give you eight pounds for the lot.'

'Eight pounds?' exclaimed Pete, but Alan recovered quickly.

'Oh, I think they're worth at least twenty,' he said calmly, but this time cheek did not pay. A ghost of a smile crossed the man's face and he said, in much the same tone as Alan, 'In that case I'll be happy to sell them back to you for twenty,' upon which Alan and Pete hastily settled for eight pounds, and left the shop jubilant.

Pete was able to get his chips then, and a great deal else besides. They only began to think about making plans when they were rounding off the feast with a knickerbocker glory apiece.

'Well,' said Alan, 'are you going to sample the garden shed tonight?'

'I can get my train now,' said Pete.

'I was afraid you'd say that.'

'Why afraid?'

'Because it would have been much more fun to keep you hidden for a few days, and smuggle food out to you, while you sneaked out every day and worked at a garage or something. I'd even fixed on a garage in my mind where I'm sure they'd take you on as a petrol pump attendant.'

Alan's eagerness was infectious. Pete thought about the plan in silence for a moment.

'It'd be daft to do it,' he said at last.

'I'm afraid you're right,' Alan agreed. 'I won't try and persuade you, because if you got found out and everything went wrong it would be my fault, and you'd never get to Kell.'

'I wouldn't be getting to Kell at all if it wasn't for you,' said Pete. 'I'd never have sold those pictures.'

'Think nothing of it,' said Alan airily. 'But I suppose while you've got the money you ought to buy your ticket and go, this very night. And anyway,' he added, getting up from the table, 'if I can't get you to my place in Pendinas, I'll make sure I come and see you in Kell.'

'However do you think you're going to manage that?' asked Pete. It sounded a splendid idea, but a most unlikely one.

Alan did not seem to think so, however. 'Why, in this motor yacht,' he said. 'I told you about that, didn't I?'

'Only just that you were hoping to go,' said Pete, 'with your brother-in-law, wasn't it?'

'That's right, and a couple of friends of his, and my sister. The boat's up in North Wales, Anglesey or somewhere. We'll be starting from there, and sailing northwards up the coast, up to Scotland among all those islands. I'll get them to land on Kell, so as I can come and see you.'

It all sounded so easy. It must be nice to live the kind of life where your relations owned ocean-going yachts and would drop you in at the island of your choice just for the asking – and yet Alan had been envious of him, Pete, for his adventurous life.

'Do you think they will?' he asked.

'I don't see why not,' said Alan. 'After all, if they want to explore the west coast of Scotland, what better way than to land on a small unknown island where they are only now building their first road? I'll be able to persuade them, don't you worry, just so long as we get as far north as that.'

'I'll be seeing you at Tom's place later on, anyway, won't I?' asked Pete. 'Even if you don't get to Kell.'

'Yeah, that's right,' said Alan. 'But I'll get to Kell.'

'Why are you so keen?' asked Pete. They were walking

down the main shopping street by now, and Alan stopped and stared unfocused into a shoe-shop window, as though beyond the plate glass and the ranks of glossy shoes he could see the island sea-scape of the Hebrides.

'I don't know,' he said. 'I want to see you've got to journey's end, I suppose. And I want to see that road your father's building, something new in a place where there's never been a road, like history in the making, isn't that it? And it's your father who is making it. Fancy cutting away turf that's been undisturbed for thousands of years, sticking your pick-axe into earth that has been hidden since the world began.'

'Only it would be a bulldozer,' said Pete. 'And there wasn't any earth when the world began, was there?'

'Oh, shush,' said Alan. 'You've got no soul.' He turned away from the window, his hand pressed to his heart and a wide grin on his face. 'And if there isn't any bike where I left it I'll have some more to say.'

It was all right, though. The yellow bicycle was still propped against the fence by the railway-sidings. They gathered it up and went on to the station and Pete bought his ticket through to Oban. He would have to change at Birmingham and at Glasgow, and the train for Birmingham was leaving in less than an hour.

For the second time that day, Pete said good-bye to a friend on the station platform, but this time when the train at last moved purposefully out of the station, it took Pete with it.

Chapter 9

IN front, blue islands, humped like whales, rose out of a blue sea towards a blue sky; behind, the mainland mountains lay lower and lower upon the ocean's rim like a grey-blue sleeping dragon; only the near objects were real, and they were startling white – the plump sheen of gulls' breasts, the lighthouse on the starboard bow, the salt-roughened paintwork on the life-belts, the iron railings, the bollards and gunwhales and all the workaday accoutrements of the little steamer.

Pete rubbed the palms of his hands up and down the blistered paint, thinking, 'Am I real?'

He was not exactly lonely, but he would have liked to have someone familiar standing beside him – Tom, say, or Alan or even Uncle Sam – who would speak to him casually, call him by his name, give him some chewing-gum or share a packet of crisps, any kind of encounter that proved he really was Peter Jenkins, the boy from Llanwern, the policeman's nephew, Tom Thomas's friend, school work quite good, hobbies football, bird-watching, and a few scrapes that were better forgotten. Not a soul on the boat knew a single thing about him, or cared. He was joined to his past by no stronger a thread than his own memory, and to his future by nothing more secure than his ability to organize himself. If he forgot himself, there was no one to remind him who he was, or what he was doing, or why he was there, floating in a blue space with the only solid land in sight gliding like whales around the horizon.

Pete drew a deep breath and took an apple out of his pocket. Immediately two or three gulls drifted nearer, squawking with gentle insistence. Pete had never seen gulls so close at hand until today, and he gazed at one of them, fascinated. The colours were as clean and clear as the sea-sky; there was a luminous quality about the astonishing whiteness of the breast, and the clear yellow of the beak and the bright spot of vermilion on the tip; and the pale eye shone as translucent and uncompassionate as the arctic sky. It moved, too, with an unstrained grace, coasting easily on wings that proclaimed they could carry it round the world and back and never tire. There was the same quality of unused strength in the little hopeful cries it was uttering, scarcely more than a croon, and yet resonant with a volume that could shriek anger or triumph across an ocean. Beneath that impeccable sheen of white plumage the body looked as solid and heavy as a wood-pigeon's, when the gull alighted on the rail, but when it lifted its arching wings and floated off into space it was truly a creature of the sea and wind.

Pete threw out the core of his apple, and the watchful gull caught it before it ever reached the waves. He still felt rather hollow, but was not sure whether it was a hungry hollowness, or the result of the long sea journey, or nervousness about what lay ahead. In any case, he could not do much about it because all his money was gone. By the time he had paid his rail fare and bought some food on the station at Glasgow, he had barely enough left for the boat ticket; what little remained he had used to buy biscuits and a sausage roll and an apple on board. His original plan to arrive at Kell as an independent traveller, ready to pay his father his share of their expenses, was gone; he would arrive hungry and broke.

Perhaps his father would not be pleased to see him at all and would put him on the next boat home, angry at the unnecessary expense. The nearer the boat moved in on the whale that was beginning to take on the solid outlines and greenness of real land, the more Pete began to realize that the meeting about to take place was no dream, but something real and not very romantic. There was nothing exciting about meeting his father on his routine visits home, when he sat quietly in the old armchair and scarcely exchanged two words with Pete; why should it be different now?

His mind wandered over the events of the past week, the fat black-haired lady on the Merthyr bus, the football match, the nightmare chase dashed across the back streets of Cardiff, and the peculiar gentle days among the railway-sidings. All these things were real all right, but they would never be more than a story to his family and school-friends back home; in time, would they be no more than a story to Pete himself? Alan was the only person likely to come to Llanwern who had also inhabited that other world, and even Alan, visiting Tygwyn as Tom's cousin, would seem a different sort of person.

He wondered if Alan would really get to Kell. He had said he would, and Alan had a way of making one believe in him, but Pete had to admit that it did not seem a very easy thing to accomplish, even for anyone as assured as Alan. He thought of the wearisome train journey all night and half the day, and the long hours ploughing through the seas that had brought him to this different world of sky and sea and islands innumerable; Cardiff and all the people in it seemed a very long way away.

The steamer hooted; people began to stir, gathering up their luggage and moving to one side of the ship. It had been very crowded as far as Mull, but most people got off at Tobermory, the Americans with their cameras, the lean sandy men in shorts with lean sandy wives and field-glasses, and the harassed family parties. Those who were left were either workmen, gathered in the bar, or crofters and housewives, treating the boat as familiarly as the village bus. Now that the workmen began to gather on deck, Pete saw that some of them carried holdalls or wore donkey jackets with the letters A.R.C.S. stencilled on them, and he realized that these were men from the road-building site where his father worked.

It crossed his mind that his father might be among them, but he was not. The sensible thing would be to go up and speak to them, saying who he was and asking how to get to the work site, but he could not bring himself to do it. He was afraid to step boldly out of his dream world. Instead, he shouldered his duffle bag and watched them from a safe distance.

The boat was fast approaching the little jetty now. There was nothing very much there – a pub, a shop, a few houses, a couple of large sheds, a crane and a patch of waste ground where two yellow earth dumpers were parked and a battered bus. On either side, close-cropped grassy headlands sloped down to a narrow ripple of rock that slid into the waves; some of them enclosed crescents of sand as pale as cream. On one, seven black cows stood dreaming; the rest were empty.

Immediately behind the houses the mountains began, billowing up into the sky; a raw new road curved away round the base of the biggest one like a frayed hem.

With a gentle bump the boat drew alongside the quay and the gang-plank was let down. Pete sidled up towards the group of workmen waiting to be allowed to disembark. When they began to stream off the boat, Pete followed, nervous and excited. One of the biggest men noticed him squeezing between the jostling passengers and made room for him.

'Come by me, then, sonny,' he said, speaking with an Irish accent, more familiar to Pete than the Scottish he had been hearing all around him since arriving in Glasgow. There were sometimes Irishmen employed as casual labour in the forestry plantations near Pete's home; they were usually friendly, talkative men.

Pete took a deep breath. 'Can you tell me how to get to the A.R.C.S. site, please?'

'Sure,' said the man, surprised. 'You take that luxury coach along with the rest of us. But for what would you be wanting to go there?'

'My dad's there; I've come to visit him,' said Pete.

'Your dad?' The man was clearly surprised. 'Now, who would he be? No, don't tell me. Might it be Jenkins you call yourself?' Pete nodded.

'Hey, lads,' the Irishman called after the men in front, 'we've got a visitor. Taff's boy, that's who this is.'

'John, my father's name is,' said Pete, confused.

'Oh, aye,' said the man. 'That's right. Jack Jenkins.'

'Quiet fellow,' added one. 'Got a wife and kid somewhere in Wales.'

'That's how I knew,' said the Irishman. 'When you spoke. I could tell, see, you come from Wales, like Taff. That's why he's Taff, him being a Welshman.'

'And *he's* Paddy,' said the younger man, with a broad cheerful face, 'coming from Ireland. And *he's* Paddy,' he added, nodding at a little wrinkled man.

'And you're Paddy,' said the wrinkled man, with a toothless grin. 'He's from Ireland, too, see?' He shook with silent laughter.

'Sure, it's a grand name,' said the first Irishman. 'And you can't have too much of a good thing, that's for certain. Only it gets a bit confusing, on times.'

'It's no worse than being a Jock,' said a small Scotsman.

'That's only now we're on a job in Scotland,' said the first Irishman, consolingly. 'All the new fellows now are Jocks. But you was always our Jock as long as I been with the firm. I remember you, when we was working in Warrington.'

'There's only one Legs,' remarked a man with an innocent leathery face.

By this time they were all climbing into the decrepit bus. It smelt of grease and stale cigarette smoke, and now the men were in an enclosed space a warm beery smell wafted around them.

'Oh, aye, there's only one Legs,' said the first Irishman. 'And that's more than enough, come Saturday nights. Fell out of a boat, didn't you, Russian trawler or something like that? But you mustn't call him Russian, he don't like it. What is it, you are, Legs?' He nudged Pete. 'He don't speak English too good,' he added confidentially.

'Lithuanian,' said Legs.

'That's right. And he's got a couple of names each longer than your arm, haven't you, Legs?' Legs nodded proudly, but did not speak. 'That's why we call him Legs.'

'I'll tell you how to know us apart,' said the little wrinkled man. He beckoned to Pete to lean across the dingy aisle. 'If he's fighting drunk, he's a Jock, and if he's roaring drunk, he's an Irishman, and if he's dead drunk, he's Legs!'

Everyone laughed a lot, and Pete, not to appear embarrassed, said, 'How can you tell if he's a Taffy?' But it was the others who seemed embarrassed, and a little silence fell upon them.

'I'll bet Taff's never been drunk in his life,' said the first Irishman, after a pause. 'I don't reckon he's the drinking sort, your dad.'

'I don't recall as I've ever seen him drunk,' said the wrinkled man, thoughtfully. 'Not now I comes to think about it.' They all appeared to be thinking about it for the first time, as though this were some puzzle to which they had never given their minds before.

'Have *you* ever seen your dad drunk?' continued the large Irishman earnestly. Pete had to admit he had not.

The younger Irishman offered a solution. 'I've heard the Welsh are very religious,' he remarked knowledgeably.

'And I am,' said Big Paddy. 'And all the Irish are. Very religious. But that's not a thing to stop me drinking, praise be to the Blessed Mother of God.'

Pete felt the conversation was getting out of his depth. It rolled back and forth around him as he sat quietly watching the dramatic landscape jolt by, and wondering about his father's place in this community.

At first the road ran along the coast; then, after crossing a river, it turned and followed the stream inland up a valley. Everything about it was so new, it could not help but be ugly. It tore across the ancient skin of the island as though it had been ripped with a giant saw. The glistening asphalt rode upon a bank of raw shale spilling out over the sheep-bitten turf, and everywhere the passage of gigantic machinery had left its mark in great deserts of dried and flattened mud.

Yet, from the limit of the road works, the mountains soared in impervious majesty, and beyond the rutted mud the stream flowed clear and sparkling among the boulders, overhung with rowan and birches and no doubt harbouring dippers and trout and blue-black beetles that could claim an unbroken pedigree back to the Ice Ages.

The road was climbing all the time, and soon the birches and rowan gave way to empty moorland. The stream ran for a while through flat marshland, and then disappeared into a ravine. The road arched away over a pass in the hills and Pete could see a reed-fringed loch immediately ahead. At first view, this one seemed more remote and isolated than any he had seen from the train but as they rounded a fold in the hills, Pete saw he was wrong. Clustered at the head of the loch, naked upon the bare mountain, stood a jumble of caravans and tin sheds and a ragged assembly of every kind of vehicle from mobile cranes to Jaguars. This must be the works site.

'There you are, then,' said Big Paddy. 'Paradise City. That's where we all live. That's where you'll find your dad.'

'Do you all live in caravans?' asked Pete.

'Mostly,' said his companion. 'Two at a time; I share with Paddy here' – he nodded at the little wrinkled man – 'and some of the young ones, they shack up in a big tin shed; boys' dormitory, we call it.'

'Who does my dad share with?' asked Pete. It suddenly occurred to him that there might not be anywhere for him to sleep.

'Oh, Taff's on his own, isn't he, Paddy?'

'Taff? Yeah, I think.' Nobody seemed very sure. Someone said they thought he had the little old blue van at the far end.

'Why?' said Pete. Perhaps his father held a special position, like being a foreman.

'No reason,' said Paddy, after a pause. 'It just happens.'

'That's right,' said the wrinkled man. 'Just happens.' The subject hung in the air, as though the last word had not been said, and no one was going to say it. Then Legs leaned forward from his seat. 'I'll tell you,' he said. 'Taff is a ver' quiet man. In that he is like me. I am a ver' quiet man.' All the men laughed.

'Och, aye, tell us some more,' said Jock.

Legs was unruffled. 'I keep my peace,' he said with simple dignity. 'And your father, I think he likes to keep his peace.'

'What piece are you on about, then?' demanded the young Paddy, grinning. 'Can I have a piece of it?'

Legs took no notice. 'I do not make fusses,' he said solemnly. 'And Taff, he does not make fusses. These fellows here, they keep on about having this van or that van or sharing with this fellow or that fellow; and when all the fussing is over, Taff and I, we get what's left. Me, I get the last bed in the boys' hut. That is because they say, "Legs is too simple to look after himself." I do not mind. I do not like to be alone. But Taff, he doesn't care. So he gets the old blue van that nobody else wants.'

'It's all right,' said Big Paddy. 'Used to leak a bit, when I was in it years ago, and it's not so modern as some, but sure your dad will have fixed it. Anyway, it's lucky for you. Does he know you're coming? Is it all fixed up?'

'Sort of,' said Pete.

'The boss don't usually like having families,' said the wrinkled man. 'Wives especially. They get to creating too much when they see the way we live.'

'There's no call for you to be worrying,' said the first Paddy, to Pete. 'Sure, your dad will have fixed it with the boss, with the site manager, that is.'

'Funny, Taff never said nothing about you coming then,' said the wrinkled man.

'No, it isn't then,' said Big Paddy, quickly. ''Cos Taff's a quiet man, we all know that. He don't go around telling everyone his private affairs. He's not like some fellows who don't know when to keep their mouths shut,' he added, with a reproving look at his mate.

Pete remembered how he had planned to send a picture-postcard to his father from Germany, to be seen on the shelf by his mates when they gathered in his caravan, and said nothing. It seemed that nobody bothered themselves about Jack Jenkins at work any more than they did in his home village.

As the old works bus creaked and jolted off the road on to the acre of flattened stone that served as a car park, Pete gazed around curiously at the peeling caravans and dingy huts that cluttered the ground like litter in a lay-by. This, then, was where he would be living – unless his father sent him straight home again. It was getting quite late, and the sun was already half cut off behind a shoulder of the mountain. Down at the far end of the loch the reeds shone golden in the sunset, but here it felt suddenly cool and grey, and a little breeze stirred the old cigarette packets among the trampled grass.

'Do you reckon Taff will be out of the canteen?' asked Big Paddy, the one who had first spoken to Pete.

'Sure to be,' said the wrinkled one. 'It's gone nine, see.'

'When does he come off work, then?' asked Pete.

'You work long hours on this job, boyo,' said Big Paddy. 'Eight till five and then all the overtime you can get. Some sites, you work all round the clock under arc lamps – shifts, you know; but out here, we just do the one shift, and then overtime as long as daylight lasts – and in the summer, that's half the night.'

'It's not living,' said the young Paddy. 'It's working and sleeping, that's all it is.'

'Come off it,' said Big Paddy. 'You do your living when you get off home with your pay packet.' He turned to Pete. 'That's your dad's van, that blue one over there. Would you be wishing for me to walk over with you?'

The other men were beginning to disperse among the ramshackle huts, each to his own van.

'No,' said Pete. 'I can find my own way. Thanks,' he added.

'Be seeing you, then,' said Paddy. 'Were you going to be staying long? I'm thinking you'll not find it very interesting. Your dad's like the rest of us – it's off to work first thing in the morning and not back till half-eight more often than not; then it's wash, and eat, and drop into bed.'

'Yeah, I know,' said Pete. He had known in a sort of way, but the reality was more telling than the idea.

'Now don't get me wrong. It's nice for us fellows to see a new face around, but I'm thinking it's not just the best place for a boy. There aren't any other kids about, and maybe there's a bit more drinking and gambling and that going on than your mother would approve of back home.' More than likely, thought Pete.

'I'm not saying nothing against any of the fellows,' went on Paddy. 'It's just that when you've been up on the hillside maybe drilling all day, or churning out rock with an excavator, when you come home you feel more like standing around with a can of beer in your hand than chasing a football around.'

'Yeah,' said Pete. 'I know. I don't expect I'll be staying long.' He walked steadily off towards the blue van, and Paddy stepped up to the door of a long green and grey one, slightly less shabby than most.

The blue caravan had its entrance on the side facing away from the site, looking down the loch; and it was when he walked round the van to find the door that he came upon his father.

He was sitting on the step of the van, looking out over the valley, relaxed and still. His eyes turned towards Pete as he came into view, blankly as first, and then a slow surprised look of recognition swept across his face.

'Pete?' he said. 'What are you doing here?' Then, with sudden urgency, 'Is it Mary? Has something happened?'

Mary? thought Pete, momentarily confused. 'Oh, yes, Mum's fine.' That was strange. Pete of course knew his mother's name was Mary, but normally his father never called her that when speaking to him – always 'your mother'. It was as though, in the sudden alarm, he had forgotten about Pete being his son.

The tenseness faded again from his father's face, but he still looked bewildered.

'What are you doing here then?' he asked.

It was the most natural question in the world, and the one Pete was expecting, but now it had actually come, he found it extremely hard to answer.

He managed a few sentences, with a good many pauses, and was just getting into the swing of it when his father interrupted him.

'Your mother's all right? You're sure of it?'

'Of course,' said Pete, slightly irritated. What did he want to keep harping on about his mother for? This was his, Pete's, adventure; his mother did not come into it. 'It's nothing to do with Mum. I tell you, it's because I was going on this trip and then there wasn't a place and ...'

'Does your mother know you're here?'

'Yes,' said Pete crossly. 'I've written to her.' He did not say when. He had in fact posted the letter in Glasgow that morning. After an uncomfortable and rather dismal night, part spent slouched in a corner and part, when his companions went off to a sleeper, stretched out, rather cold on the narrow seat, he had woken early and as the train rattled through the mist-hung lowlands he had tried to compose the letter that he knew he must write. After putting, 'Dear Mum,' it was a long time before he wrote anything more at all. Then he started a sentence, only to scratch it out again. In the end, at the third attempt, he dashed down a very hurried note, simply saying he had got into trouble at school and couldn't go to Germany and had run away to Kell. He sealed it quickly, thinking the train was about to arrive in Glasgow, but he was wrong; for nearly another hour he had fiddled indecisively with the letter, wishing he hadn't used the phrase 'run away', and wondering whether he had time to open it and start again. Then, suddenly, they were there, and it was too late to alter anything.

Mr Jenkins had relapsed into silence, and Pete skated on rather quickly now with his story, leaving out the reason for his exclusion from the trip. His father did not seem interested in the details.

'How are you going to get home again?' he asked after a while.

Pete was once more thrown off his stride. He had not got to the end of his story.

'I thought ...' he started. 'I've been thinking ... Couldn't I stop and come back with you when you next come home?'

'Week on Friday, that'll be,' said his father slowly. He paused, then added, 'We'll ask your mother.'

Suddenly the niggling crossness swelled into a mountain of anger. 'Why do you always have to ask *her* everything?' Pete shouted. 'You're my father, aren't you? Why've you always got to let Mum run everything? Mum and Uncle Sam,' he added, his voice trailing off into a furious mutter.

'Do I?' asked his father, mildly. He appeared to consider the matter. Then he got up slowly. 'You'll be hungry, I expect. Got any money left?'

'I'm all right,' said Pete. 'I had enough to get something on the boat.'

'And now you're skint.'

'Yes.'

'Canteen's closed now, but I expect I've got a bit of something in the van.' He led the way inside, and Pete followed, curious despite himself.

It was smaller than he had expected, and very shabby, but clean and tidy. His father lit the gas ring and put the kettle on, then stood, considering.

'Your mother will be worrying to know whether you've got here safely, shouldn't wonder,' he remarked. 'We'd better send her a telegram; or maybe we could ring your Uncle Sam. There's a phone we can use at the site office.' He paused. 'I can't say as I've ever used it myself, though lots of the men do. But maybe the boss'd help us. Unless you are good at working them things?'

'I dare say I could do,' said Pete dispiritedly. Was this slow, muddled man the father he had come so far to seek? 'It would be better not to ring tonight though. She may not get my letter till tomorrow, and so she'll still be thinking I'm in Germany.'

'How's that, then?' asked Mr Jenkins, and Pete realized his father had not really taken in half of what he had been telling him.

'I *told* you,' he began irritably.

'It's a lot to take in,' said his father, 'at the end of a hard day's work. Bacon and egg?'

'Yes, please.' Pete felt ashamed of himself for being so cross. His father had uttered no word of reproof, nor made him feel in any way unwelcome.

'I generally eat in the canteen in the evenings,' said Mr Jenkins, 'but I cook my own breakfast in the mornings, and on my half-days and that. There's another bed over there where you can sleep.' He nodded at a threadbare settee. 'It's all right this weather, but in a heavy storm the rain comes in a bit at that end. Think you'll be all right?'

'Yeah, fine.' Pete watched his father ladling the bacon and egg on to a plate with careful deliberation. It smelt delicious, and Pete's spirits rose. His father watched him eat in silence for a while, and then said, 'It were a bit of a surprise, seeing you come round the corner of the van like that. Takes a bit of getting used to.' There was another long pause. Pete busied himself with his eating.

'Why did you come, then?' asked his father at length.

'It was this school trip,' began Pete, resigned to starting all over again.

'I know that,' said Mr Jenkins. 'You told me. They hadn't got a place for you. But why did you want to come here?'

Pete munched away, thinking. 'I dunno,' he said at last. 'I don't see much of you at home, do I?'

Mr Jenkins looked at him steadily, and his face broke into a slow smile.

'You're not missing much,' he commented. 'Most of your friends've got dads a lot smarter than me, I shouldn't wonder. You'd better make the most of your Uncle Sam.'

'Huh,' said Pete. He grinned back. 'Can I stay, now I've come?'

'Aye,' said his father, adding, with a trace of slow mischief, 'if your mother lets you.' He poured them each out a cup of hot strong tea. 'It'll be nice to have someone to talk to, for a change,' he said, carefully passing the full cup to Pete. 'Help yourself to sugar.'

The tea was delicious, but too hot for Pete to drink quickly. As he sat sipping cautiously and waiting for it to cool, Mr Jenkins emptied his cup with a few deep steady gulps, and proceeded to take down some neatly-folded sheets and blankets out of a locker and make up a bed on the couch. Pete felt his eyelids begin to slide down as sudden weariness swept through him.

'I generally go to bed about now,' said Mr Jenkins. 'And it looks as if you're ready, too. I'll have to see the boss about you staying here before I go to work in the morning.' He picked up the kettle and went out. Pete could see him through the window, walking in his stiff long-limbed way to a stand-pipe down the alley-way. He carefully filled the kettle and came back into the van with it and set it on the gas.

'That's for the dishes,' he said. 'We'll leave it to hot now while I show you the wash-house. There'll not be many there yet.'

They walked down together in the cool dusk to a long hut that looked and smelt like the boys' cloakroom at school, only worse. Pete did not reckon he needed much of a wash and he was soon back at the van where he found his father just about to wash up. They did the job together, and then while Pete slid readily into bed Mr Jenkins gathered up his towel and washing things and went off to the wash hut.

He was gone a long time, and Pete could imagine him carefully and conscientiously scrubbing off the grime of the day's work, unmoved by his bleak surroundings. This kind of living was all right for school, thought Pete, or for a holiday, but his father had to live that way for eleven months of the year. His eye ran around the dingy interior of the van. There was no clutter of any sort, no ornament or book, not even a radio. Only in one corner a faded snapshot was pinned to the wall, of his mother in her best Sunday suit holding a bundled baby. Himself, he supposed, probably at his christening. A newspaper, folded small, lay on the shelf together with a bottle of ink and some notepaper and envelopes. Near by lay a letter addressed in his mother's handwriting. Nothing more.

Mark would be content to live as simply as this, but Mark had Della and Thursday and the dream of his painting. Pete's father spent most of his life in this austere way without anything further as his goal – except, perhaps, that long, long journey every few weeks, alone in the ancient A.30, for the reward of three evenings sitting in his own armchair at his own hearth, accepting as a treat something that most householders took as the bread and butter of their lives.

Pete sighed, puzzled by his own thoughts. It was not, in fact, that his father lived a life very different from the one he had pictured; a little lonelier, a little harder, a little less luxurious, but not so very different. Yet this reality was a world away from the dream. He had come all this way to discover a father he had never learnt to know, and he had discovered him, but not as the mysterious romantic figure he had imagined, and yet . . . and yet . . .

Pete was almost asleep when his father came back in. He watched him through half-closed eyes moving methodically about the little caravan, hanging up his towel, putting his clothes, tidily folded, into a locker. As he reached to turn out the gas lamp, the fading glow from the mantle lit up his lean, quiet face, and the image hung on in the darkness and in Pete's tired mind until, in a moment, he fell asleep.

Chapter 10

THE next morning, while Mr Jenkins went to see the Site Manager, Pete bought a picture postcard showing five views of Oban at the site shop – he had to ask his father for the money – and wrote to his mother a second time. This one was much easier. He just said, 'Have got here safely and am staying with Dad in his caravan. He says can I come home with him next week. Everything is O.K. Love from Pete.'

He showed it to his father when he returned. Mr Jenkins took a long time to read it. Then he nodded, and said, 'You'd best say I'll write myself this evening,' so Pete added a P.S. to that effect.

During the next week he did not see much of his father, but he enjoyed their quiet breakfasts together in the early morning, and seeing him step down from the old bus each evening, stiff-legged and powdered with stone dust, and watching his face break into a slow smile when he saw Pete waiting for him by the van.

Pete told him, eventually, all about Bongo's and the troubles that had followed. All his father said was, 'Bit of a spot you got yourself into.' He never asked Pete any questions or tried to organize his life for him, but listened seriously and attentively, sitting on the caravan step each evening while Pete wandered about telling him of the day's events or of things that had happened at home. He gave Pete two pounds so that he could get his own meals during the day while the men were out, and left it to Pete to decide what to spend it on.

The works site held little attraction for Pete during the long days when the mountains and streams beckoned. After his father had gone off to work he would go down to the canteen and buy food and take off into the countryside. The first day or two he bought lots of sweets and crisps and fizzy pop, but then he changed over to meat pies and sliced loaves from which he concocted sandwiches with peculiar fillings. He explored the loch, finding a late gull's nest with newly-hatched speckled young; he followed the stream down to the sea, and discovered for himself one of those little secret cream-coloured bays he had seen from the boat. Here the sea was not separated from the countryside by the kind of no-man's land he was accustomed to – promenades and buildings, or acres of sand-dunes or an expanse of stony foreshore – but the sweet inland turf, gay with innumerable daisies and buttercups, spilt right down to the very verge of the ocean; one moment the brook ran through a peaty bog full of orchids and sundew and all the flowers of the marsh, and the next it cut a clean channel through the bright and barren sands. He entered up the birds he knew, or guessed at, in his book, he scrambled over the rocks and waded in the shallow waves. It would have been a beautiful place to go swimming, but that was something Pete just did not feel like doing without company. Suddenly, earnestly, he wished Tom were with him. Or Alan? He stared out over the waves. It just did not seem possible that Alan should ever find his way into this far-off sea.

It was the same on the mountains. Pete looked up at the great peaks around the site and decided he would climb to the top of the nearest one, but when he got half-way up, he changed his mind – not because he lacked the strength or the agility to cope with the steep slopes, but these mountains were very different from those he knew at home. They were so huge, so rocky, and so uninhabited. In the Welsh hills, farm tracks infiltrated up every cwm to lonely farmhouses whose owners kept a kind of loose authority over the grassy uplands above them, and there was no place where you might not expect to come upon a farmer and his dogs rounding up the sheep. But here the upper slopes formed a world quite outside man's rule. Even the hardy sheep scarcely penetrated, and if they did it was on equal, unprotected terms with the foxes and ravens and the wild red deer that Pete came upon round a shoulder of rock. It was an exciting place, but too strange to stay in for long without a companion.

The thrill of seeing the deer made Pete most aware of his loneliness. For some time he watched them grazing, undetected because of a lucky combination of wind and shadow. Then the stag raised his magnificent antlered head and stared towards him, stamped, softly at first and then more urgently, so that the herd looked up and followed the direction of his gaze, their soft nostrils flared to sift the air for scent. Pete kept still as the rock under his hand until they returned to their grazing, but the stag remained a long time watching intently and at last began to lead his does unhurriedly to higher ground. It was at moments like these that Pete longed for Alan to share the thrills of discovery with him, but already his Cardiff adventures began to seem as unreal as a dream and Alan a story-book figure who only existed for him when he was alone.

Apart from the football match, he did not talk about any of his Cardiff experiences to the men at the site. Unconsciously, he was afraid that if he did, his own vision of things and people would be overlaid with a reflection of the way his audience would see it; like laying a sheet of tissue paper over a delicate drawing and tracing the outlines with a thick black crayon in a childish hand. He said nothing, and reaped a private dream world where the images remained bright and intact, but ever more remote from reality. The only link was the fading bruise upon his cheek-bone.

Soon he left off thinking about the possibility of Alan's arrival, and even the knowledge that he would see him later on at Tygwyn was tempered by the thought that his friend would probably appear a much more ordinary and altogether different boy in those homely surroundings.

There was a youngish engineer on the site who turned out to be a keen ornithologist and took an interest in Pete after he had met him over the weekend exploring the marsh at the end of the loch and entering birds in his little book. He was rather too expert for Pete, but it was pleasant to have someone to whom he could talk about his hobby, and when he had a few spare hours Mr Coates, the engineer, would take Pete on bird-watching excursions. He was actually the man in charge of the explosives used in making the roadway, and when, a couple of days later, there were some big blasting operations to be undertaken, Mr Coates asked Pete if he would like to spend the day with the workmen and see how it was done. 'So long as you observe the safety precautions like everybody else and don't make a nuisance of yourself,' he said.

In fact, he told Pete, safety precautions were much less complicated here on Kell than anywhere else he had known, because of the isolation of the site.

'Nobody can get here except up the road we are building,' he said, 'unless they tramp over five or six miles of open hillside, and even then there's only about two crofts they can come from, and the crofters there know all about our operations. We used always to post a couple of men on the far side of whatever rocks we were blasting in case anybody came up the stream, where we mightn't see them, instead of down over the shoulder of the mountain where they'd see the red flag anyway; but then we found the buildings we'd seen at the foot of the valley, down by the sea, were long since deserted, and there just isn't anybody living on the island who could come up that way, so we don't bother. We drive the sheep off first – and the birds,' he added with a grin.

'And the deer?' said Pete.

'It's not likely they'd stay within a couple of miles of us,' said Mr Coates, laughing. 'We don't exactly go about our job like deer-stalkers.'

Pete discovered, for the first time, that it was his father who, with Mr Coates, actually set the charges. It seemed strange that two such quiet-loving men should be responsible for anything so noisy as rock-blasting, but then, as Mr Coates said, all road-making was noisy, and this was the only part of it that wasn't continuously so. 'Things like the earth-diggers or the drills go on and on, but with a charge, you get this tremendous crash, and then, after the reverberations die away, a most beautiful silence.'

First a number of holes were drilled in the sections of rock to be demolished, and then these were filled with explosive, which was connected up to a series of timed fuses in such a way that the two men had ample time to get away, and then each charge went off one after the other, with a short interval in between. Pete's father always knew exactly how many were due to go off, and none of the men were allowed to go forward until every charge had exploded with a dull thud and a cloud of dust and rubble. This was just the kind of simple yet highly responsible job for which Mr Jenkins was best suited.

Clearing away the resultant debris took the men the rest of the morning, and then they all stopped for a dinner-break. Pete enjoyed lounging with the men on the sunny hillside, munching thick sandwiches and feeling accepted as one of the team.

After dinner, Mr Coates and Mr Jenkins went forward and set another series of charges in the rocks. There was a great overhanging outcrop which had to be got rid of.

'Can't do it all at once, I shouldn't think,' said Mr Coates. 'We'll set the first batch well apart and see if we can break it up a bit into smaller sections, and then we can tackle those one at a time.'

The charges were set, and Coates and Jenkins strode back, cool and unhurried, to join the men watching on the hillside.

And then, young Paddy pointed, and they all saw the figure of a boy running up the gully on the far side, straight towards the place where the last charge had been fixed in the rock face.

There were cries of astonishment. 'The dam' fool!' 'What does he think he's up to?' 'Where the devil did he spring from?'

'Hi!' yelled Coates at the top of his voice. The boy looked up towards them, stood still immediately under the outcrop, and waved cheerily.

It was then that Pete realized who it was. It was Alan.

Between one heart-beat and the lagging next, he saw his friend waving gaily beneath the deadly rock, cradled between the steep mountains under a smiling sky, he felt rather than saw the horror-struck tenseness of the workmen around him, he heard Coates shouting meaningless words, his voice hoarse with fear and urgency. He felt all those things, too, horror and fear and urgency, and above that, a particular horror because Alan was his friend; but he also felt a strange sort of delight, because Alan had come like he said he would, contentment even, because here was proof of his friendship, and glory, too, because Alan had swept in on a gale of adventure in a way that befitted him.

But then his heart beat again, and the only feeling left in him was horror.

'You ... are ... in ... great ... danger!' Mr Coates was shouting. 'There will be explosions at any moment. You must run!'

For a long long second Alan stood still, waiting for the words to drift down the valley to him. Then he seemed to understand, because he suddenly began to leap towards them.

'Not that way,' muttered Big Paddy, for that was the way the line of charges ran. Mr Coates had the same thought.

'The ... other way!' he yelled, waving frantically. '*Go the other way!*'

It was a mistake to have shouted, because Alan, clattering

over the stones and breathing heavily, obviously could not make out the words, and stopped again to listen.

'Hurry!' shouted Pete, and seeing that Alan came on towards them he made a move as though to go and meet him.

Mr Coates put out his hand and pulled him back. 'Don't be . . .'

But at that moment the first charge went off. Alan seemed to be thrown flat on his face before the rocks began to fly; then the dust-cloud hid him from view. When it cleared, his body could be seen lying still where it had fallen.

A ripple of movement ran through the watchers, but Mr Coates spoke sharply. 'No!' he said. 'It would be suicide, and it wouldn't save him.'

The men shifted uneasily, their eyes on the still figure. They all knew the next charge was due to go off at any moment, and it was a stage nearer than the first.

'Somebody must go,' muttered Paddy. 'The poor dam' fool.'

'Not you or anyone,' said Coates, and he tightened his hold on Pete.

'Look!' exclaimed Legs. 'Down there! It's Taff!'

Every eye followed the pointing finger. A man was striding over the uneven ground away down on the right; he was not running, but he was covering the ground at an enormous rate. The lean figure in dark shirt and overalls certainly looked like Mr Jenkins. Pete at once swung round to look at the spot where he had last seen his father, standing in rock-like calm slightly away from the main group, timing in his mind when each explosion was due to go off. He had gone.

No one had seen him go. He must have moved off as soon as young Paddy had pointed out the boy, so matter-of-factly that his departure caught no eye, fixed as they all were upon the distant figure. He was now well over half-way towards him, and as they watched he dropped deliberately to the ground. An instant later the second explosion roared off, accompanied by another rain of rocks. At once, Jenkins got to his feet again and moved on at the same steady pace.

'He knew just when that was coming,' murmured Coates.

'How did he know? Just then?' whispered Pete.

Paddy glanced round at him, as if out of a dream. 'Mother of God,' he muttered. 'That's Taff's boy.' He turned to Pete. 'Timing explosions, that's your dad's job. He's got a clock in his head. There isn't nobody more likely to succeed than your dad.'

Mr Coates' hand dropped on Pete's arm, kindly, but firm as iron. 'That's right,' he said. 'He knows what he's doing, and it won't help to have anyone messing it up.'

Alan still lay as before, apparently untouched by the second explosion, but the third would be nearer, and the fourth charge was sunk in the rock almost directly above him.

Jenkins moved steadily on.

'He'll not get there and away before the next one,' said Jock.

'How many more?' asked young Paddy.

'Six in all,' replied Coates, not taking his hand from Pete's shoulder. 'Four more to go.'

As he spoke, Jenkins, now only a few yards from Alan, crouched behind a shelf of rock and for the third time the air was torn with thunder and hurtling rocks. A sigh went through the watchers, of sheer amazement at the uncanny timing.

Then, 'He's had his chips,' said Jock.

Not Dad, thought Pete, as the lean figure rose up and moved purposely forward; but then he saw that fresh rocks lay scattered around Alan, partly hiding him from view.

'Get to hell out of it, Taff,' breathed Big Paddy. 'Leave the fellow be.'

'You've got a hope,' said wrinkled Paddy. 'Or else you don't know Taff.'

In less than a dozen strides Jenkins had reached Alan and lifted the limp form on to his shoulder. Then he turned and walked steadily away from them, a straining control evident in every line of his taut body.

It was the obvious thing to do, because it meant he would be getting away from the line of the unexploded charges instead of walking almost into them, and yet for some reason it was unexpected. Pete had assumed he would have struggled straight back towards the waiting group, so that they could meet him half-way and share his load.

It seemed to surprise the others, too, but almost at once Coates grasped the situation.

'Paddy,' he said, to the big man. 'Don't let anyone stir till the other three charges have all gone off. I'm going up around. You come with me, Jock; you may be needed.' He stopped as Taff, for the first time, broke into a staggering run, and dived out of sight behind a bit of a mound, rolling the body on to the ground ahead of him as he did so. Almost at once there was another roar and the whole of the rock face above them seemed to split away from the mountain, hang for an unbelievable moment in space, and then crash in folds upon the place where Alan had been lying.

Because of the distance, and the fact that the rock wall fell in one piece, the picture reached them in utter silence; but then the echoing crash caught up with it, investing the sight with a grim reality. Of Taff and Alan there was no sign; the rock fall, smouldering with powdered dust, seemed to envelop the whole area, and hid the farther ground from view.

Coates looked down at Pete, with a touch of uncertainty. 'No point in your coming,' he said. 'You'd better stay here with Paddy.'

'I'm coming,' said Pete. Jock had already set off across the upper slopes and Coates released his hold on Pete.

'O.K.,' he said. 'Keep by me, then.' They ran, across the uneven ground, making a detour round the outcrop. It was exhausting and slippery running across the face of so steep a gradient. Immediately above the outcrop there was a stretch of invitingly level turf, but Mr Coates made them keep well above that, clambering over shaly rock and slippery eroded soil. Coates was evidently fit, as well as an experienced mountaineer, and Pete, for all his agility and youth, found it stretched his heart and lungs to keep up with him. They both soon overtook Jock, running with great gasping intakes of breath.

When the fifth explosion erupted, almost directly below them, they hardly paused. In any case, they were now cut off from what was going on below by the remnants of the outcrop itself. But after it had passed, Coates allowed himself to work sharply down the gradient; the sixth, and last, explosion, would be well back behind them by the time it went off.

Coates began to look about him as he ran, searching for any sign of life. Both Pete's father and the boy he had gone to rescue seemed to have disappeared off the face of the earth – unless their bodies lay hidden beneath the smoking pile of rubble which they could now begin to view from the farther side.

As they paused, looking about in some uncertainty, a rattle of stones made them swing round, but it was only Jock, skidding down the slope behind them. The next instant, Pete felt himself picked up and flung to the ground as though by a giant hand, and as he hit the turf he heard the thunder of the last charge exploding. At the moment of falling he glimpsed Mr Coates tottering backwards with flailing arms through a whirling arc of mountain, like a baby trying out its first steps, and a moment later Jock slithered heavily into him.

'Are ye all richt?' gasped Jock.

'Yeah,' said Pete, dazed not so much by his fall as by astonishment at the unseen power that could shake him so.

'Well, that's the last,' observed Mr Coates, picking himself up. He stared at the battered landscape in silence. A trickle of small stones suddenly rolled down a gully, making them jump.

In front of them lay the jumbled heaps of rock. Below, the

ground dropped away into a little ravine, at the bottom of which an unseen brook could be heard babbling unconcernedly away.

'Pete,' said Mr Coates. 'You go and see if anyone is down in that gully, while Jock and I look – look along this upper part.'

Pete knew what that meant. The only place on the upper part where anyone could be hidden was under the fallen rock, and Mr Coates did not want him to see what they might find there. Jock had been called along because he was the First Aid expert in the gang, but it did not look as though there was going to be anything he could do. Pete turned dully away and picked his way along a sheep track into the bed of the gully. Although he did not expect to find anything he was glad to be alone.

But he was not alone. He rounded a knob of granite, and there was his father standing in the stream and pouring water from his cupped hands over Alan's face. The boy was lying propped against a slab of rock, groaning slightly and turning his head from side to side.

Pete gave a sort of strangled gulp and his father looked up.

'Ah,' he said, 'you've not been long. See if you can find Jock – he's the man for this job.'

Pete wanted to cry out, 'Dad, I thought you were dead!', to rush down and clutch at his worn dungarees, to feel him and know he was alive, but his father went on methodically bathing Alan's head and Pete knew none of that was necessary. Those were the same careful hands he had watched, filling a kettle or writing a letter to Mum. But what of Alan?

'Is he going to be all right?' he whispered.

'Most likely,' said his father. 'But get Jock.'

'Yeah,' he said. 'I can do that easy. He's just up here,' and he scrambled back up the slope. He hurried not because there was a real need to hurry but because he knew if he stopped to let his feelings overrun him he would want to cry.

The other two men were clambering about the fallen rock, their faces hopeless. Mr Coates turned to hear what Pete was shouting.

'They're all right. They're here. Down by here!'

The two men turned and ran at once down into the little gully, but Pete stayed to await the arrival of the other men and tell them the news. In a while he would want to go back to see how Alan was, but not just yet. Not until Jock could say how he was.

He explained what had happened to Big Paddy and the rest, and while they were still clustered round, Mr Coates re-appeared.

'Taff's all right,' he said to Paddy, 'but the boy should have a doctor. He's had a bang on the head, and though Jock doesn't think it's serious, it could be.'

'I seen to that,' said Paddy. 'As soon as you'd gone I sent young Paddy back to the camp to telephone. I told him to take your car – I hope that's all right.'

Pete began to climb back down, but slowly. He had not yet told anyone that Alan was not an unknown trespasser but his friend come to look for him. Now that the danger was apparently past he felt strangely unfriendly towards him.

'He's my friend,' he said, really to persuade himself, but he spoke aloud into the little silence around the injured boy, and several of the men turned to him in surprise.

'You know him then?' asked Jock, and Pete said yes, he did, and all the time he felt embarrassed and cold towards Alan, and angry. He did not want to say any more, but of course they were all waiting then for him to go on, so grudgingly and in a muddled sort of way he had to try and explain how it was that Alan came to be there. He began to feel that it wasn't only Alan's fault, but his as well, that his father had so nearly got killed.

But Mr Jenkins' mind was working along quite a different tack.

'It just goes to show,' he said. 'Next time, we'll make sure we get the warning flags up, proper.'

'Ah, surely,' said Paddy, 'but everyone on the island knows about the blasting, and there's notices up plain for all to see along the road and all. He must have been walking around with his eyes shut.'

'Not if he came straight up from the sea on that side,' said Mr Coates, 'and maybe that's just what he did, if he came by boat. There's quite a decent mooring for a boat down in that cove, now I come to think about it.'

'But who would think about it?' said Paddy.

'I should have,' said Mr Coates quietly, but no one heard him because Alan began to stir and look around. His eyes travelled vaguely over the circle of unknown faces unfocused at first so that he passed Pete without any sign of recognition, but a puzzled frown creased his brow, and the wandering eyes moved back again until they rested a second time on Pete.

'Take it easy, son, you're all right,' said Big Paddy encouragingly.

The eyes moved to trace the voice, and then came back again to Pete. Gradually they steadied and cleared. 'Pete?' he murmured, and then, with a good deal of the old certainty, 'Pete!'

'Yeah,' said Pete. His voice sounded husky, so he cleared his throat and tried again. 'Yeah, I'm here.'

'Pete' – there was a puzzled, almost disbelieving note in the voice – 'Pete, what happened? Did somebody shoot me?'

Everyone smiled and the tension eased.

'Not quite,' said Coates. 'You walked straight into a blasting operation. We had just set charges in the rocks above here.'

Alan thought about this, and put a hand gingerly to his head. 'How was I to know?' he said. He tried to sit up and look around him, but then he had to close his eyes and lean his head back against the rock. He was so still and pale that

Pete thought he had passed out, but soon the dark lively eyes opened again and he said, with the trace of a smile, 'It's almost as good an adventure as one of yours.'

For a moment, Pete felt another flicker of anger. It was quickly gone but it left him with nothing to say. Alan really was not to blame for what had happened, but it irked Pete that all the danger and horror of those few minutes between the first explosion and the last should be reduced in Alan's mind to the level of a good adventure. And how could he ever tell him otherwise?

Fortunately, it was not left to him to try. Big Paddy undertook the telling, and poured out all the detail and the drama of it with as much enthusiasm as Alan listened.

'Which is Taff, then?' he asked, looking from face to face.

'Taff's – where are you, then, Taff? Well, where's Taff got to?' Big Paddy looked around, and so did the others. Taff was not there.

Big Paddy went off to look for him and the other men began to move away, too, to stand and talk to each other about the event, or to climb up and examine the debris and see if there was any sign of the doctor arriving. Jock and Mr Coates stayed near by to keep an eye on Alan, leaving Pete on his own beside him.

'I got here,' said Alan.

'Yeah, you did and all. Where's your boat?'

Alan waved an unnaturally languid hand down the valley. 'In a cove down there. We were in the main harbour yesterday, and could see the new road heading off in this direction, and I thought it would be fun if I could walk up from the other side and surprise you!'

'Well, you did that all right,' admitted Pete.

'Surprised myself, too,' said Alan. The laugh brought a slight frown back to his face.

'Does your head hurt a lot?' asked Pete.

'Not if I keep still,' said Alan. 'Not a lot, anyway, considering. Who's this chap Taff, Pete, who rescued me? He must be very brave. I wish I'd seen it all happen. Boy! What a waste, to be lying there unconscious all the time.'

'My dad's the one they call Taff.'

'And you were able to see it all. It's always you that gets the adventures, even when it's me who . . .' Pete's words at last caught up on him. 'Your dad? You mean it was your father who rescued me?'

Pete nodded.

'Hey, that's marvellous!' Alan's pale face became quite pink as he thought about it. 'I mean, that's just how it should be, isn't it? That's just how I knew he would be from what you said.'

'What I said? What did I say?'

'You know, when we were talking the day of the football match about him building this road in Kell, and then when I saw you again and you told me you were running away to join him, I knew then he must be someone special, for you to want to do that.'

Pete was silent. Had he really given Alan the impression that his dad was 'someone special'? Or had Alan just imagined it because that was how he wanted it to be? Or both of them had wanted it to be?

'No,' Pete said. 'That was wrong. He isn't someone special. Not the way you mean, or the way I meant either. Most times, he's a bit thick, really he is.'

He had spoken without thinking, but as soon as it was out he thought, in surprise, that's true, too. It was something he would never have admitted before, but now he not only knew it to be true but knew that it did not matter if it was true. It did not stop him from feeling proud and fond of his father. Mum knew that, too.

'I don't believe that,' said Alan.

'But it's true,' Pete said, and then stopped. It wasn't any

use trying to convince Alan. He wanted his ten-foot hero, and that was that.

'Is that him?' asked Alan in a slightly awestruck voice. Pete turned and saw his father climbing down the bank with a coat over his arm.

'Thought you might get cold waiting,' said Mr Jenkins, 'so I went to get this old coat from the bus.' He laid it over Alan.

'I'm all right, thanks,' said Alan. He blushed a little. 'Thanks to you,' he added.

'It's warm when you're working but you soon get chill sitting still,' said Mr Jenkins.

Alan was not to be diverted. 'That big Irishman told me all about it – how you rescued me, I mean.'

Taff regarded him solemnly. 'He can make a good story out of anything, that Paddy,' he commented. He thought for a moment, then added, as though it was something that had just occurred to him, 'Maybe it was a bit risky, like, now I come to think of it. But we shouldn't ever have let up on putting out the warnings.'

Mr Coates had joined the group. 'You're right there, Taff, and that was my fault,' he said. 'But there's one thing I wish you'd tell me. How did you know to a split second when each explosion was to go off?'

Jenkins considered. 'I dunno, now you ask me,' he said, slowly scratching an ear. 'Instinct, I suppose. Explosives can be tricky things if you don't know the ways of them. But they're just like anything else; if you knows the ways of them you're safe enough.'

Pete thought of the way he had been lifted up and dropped on the ground like a scrap of waste-paper; he did not think explosives were like anything else.

Just then the doctor arrived and examined Alan. He did not think there was much wrong with him, but said he should go into the hospital at Oban for a couple of days' rest and observation, and arranged that he would take him down to the port in his car and put him to bed at the little guest house near the landing-stage. Meanwhile Pete was to walk down the valley to the cove with Mr Coates and explain to Alan's family what had happened so that they could sail round in their boat and collect him and take him to the mainland.

They set off down the isolated valley to the sea.

'You won't forget today in a hurry,' said Mr Coates after they had walked a little way in silence. 'I'm glad it has ended all right.' He paused, as though there was more to be said than that but did not know quite how to say it. Pete scrambled on down, not knowing what to say either.

'One thing,' said Mr Coates eventually. 'You'll have something to tell them at home. And mind you do,' he added, 'because I bet your father wouldn't say anything.'

Pete grinned. 'I'll do that,' he said. But he knew he would never be able to tell it as it had really happened. It needed a Big Paddy or an Alan for that, and it was unlikely that Big Paddy would ever come to Llanwern, and Alan would never know the truth of those few minutes when he lay unconscious.

'Your home is somewhere near Aberafon, isn't it?' asked Mr Coates suddenly.

'Yes,' said Pete, surprised that he should have heard of the place.

'Then you'll be having your father working a lot nearer home before long,' said the engineer. 'There's a new contract we'll be starting on as soon as this is done, building a new bridge and trunk road improvements in your part of the world. We'll be based at Aberafon. I don't suppose your father knows about it yet; I've only just heard myself. You'll be able to tell him.'

Pete said, 'That'll be great.' His mind was just beginning to take in the implications of this unexpected news, when Mr Coates said, 'That must be the boat.'

They had rounded a corner and saw the cove clearly below them, with the yacht riding at anchor a short way from the shore, and a dinghy pulled up on the beach. As they got nearer they could make out four figures sunning themselves on the sands – two women in bikinis and two bronzed young men. It was an unexpected sight on the remote beach, a whiff of Barry Island in a spot usually inhabited only by seals and sea birds.

'This isn't going to be an easy interview,' said Mr Coates in a tone grown suddenly nervous, and indeed he was right. Once Alan's sister, a dark girl not unlike her brother, had been reassured that he was not seriously hurt she was calm and pleasant enough, but her husband was inclined to be truculent. Somebody was definitely to blame, his attitude seemed to say, and more than likely it was Mr Coates. Phrases like 'gross inefficiency', 'legal implications' and 'compensation' kept cropping up in his remarks, and Pete was reminded of the time – was it really only a week ago? – when he stood in the derelict sidings watching Mark and Della being harangued by the peppery railway official. Another scene, one that he had almost forgotten, but still rankled when he remembered it, rose up in his mind – himself being casually condemned by his headmaster for his part in the tobacconist's raid.

'It's not just schoolboys that get into hot water,' he suddenly thought, and with the thought, that little bubble of rancour tucked away inside him rose harmlessly to the surface and burst.

The story told and the arrangements completed, a rather silent Mr Coates led the way back up the valley. It was Pete who did all the talking.

'It makes you mad, doesn't it?' he remarked cheerfully, 'when something's a bit your fault so you can't really argue and yet you know it's not really as bad as people make out. Rows at school are always like that.'

'I suppose so,' said Mr Coates, a little taken aback.

'If I'd told you about Alan saying he might come, would it have made any difference? I mean about putting up the warning flag and that?'

'I'm not sure. Could have done, I suppose.'

'I really wasn't expecting him,' said Pete truthfully. 'I mean, I thought he was just talking. Not at first, but afterwards, I mean. I only met him last week, in Cardiff.'

'Oh, yes?' It was a rather absent-minded reply, but it was enough for Pete. Now that the excitement was over, he just wanted to talk. He talked all the way back, about all the people he had met since he left home and the things he had done, and about his life at home and what it was like to have a father who was never there and why he had wanted to come to Kell. It all came tumbling inconsequentially out as he puffed and scrambled up the rocky dingle. 'Oh, yes?' said Mr Coates occasionally. It was only when they were back in sight of the workmen that he said anything else.

'Your mother must be a great talker,' he remarked.

'Why?' said Pete.

'Well, Taff's one of the quietest men I know; you must have got it from somewhere.' Pete looked at him uncertainly for a moment, and then he saw that he was laughing. 'Tell you what,' Mr Coates went on, 'I'll take you over to Oban tomorrow to see your friend Alan and then you can make sure he's all right. He'll probably be back on his smart yacht in a couple of days, and I suppose you'll be going back then, too. Doesn't your father start his holidays on Saturday?'

'Yeah,' said Pete. 'He'll be taking me home then. We start off on Friday evening after work, and sleep in the car for a few hours to break the journey.'

When he got back, there was a letter from his mother. Pete stood in the caravan and looked at the envelope addressed in the familiar handwriting, waiting for his father to come and open it. He had stopped on his way back from the bus to rinse his hands under the tap, as he always did after the dusty day's work.

'There's a letter from Mum,' said Pete, holding it out. Mr Jenkins dried his hands thoroughly before taking it, then took a knife from the drawer in his neat slow way and slit open the envelope. Pete watched his face, but it betrayed nothing.

'She says there's a postcard for you,' he said at length. He peered back into the envelope. 'I suppose this is it. From Tom, she says.'

Pete took it and studied the picture. It was of Cologne Cathedral. Then he turned it over, and read, in Tom's scrawly handwriting, 'We are having a good time, but I wish you were here. I hope life isn't too boring at home. I wasn't sick on the boat. Yesterday we went over this Cathedral. See you next week. Love Tom.'

No, thought Pete. Life's been a lot of things, but not boring. He looked back at his father, to see if he had finished reading the letter from Mum. He was folding it carefully and putting it back in its envelope.

'What does she say?'

'Do you want to see?' Mr Jenkins seemed surprised, but he unfolded the letter again and handed it to Pete. 'Seems she's been fretting about you a bit,' he commented. 'She says to tell you she got your letter.'

'Dear Jack,' Pete read. 'I was very glad to get your telegram and letter after I heard from Pete. That was a bit of a shock, I can tell you.' Good, thought Pete, at least she had not heard from anyone else that he was not in Germany before his letter arrived. 'Will you be sure to bring him home on Saturday. How did he get to Scotland, that's what I want to know, and why didn't he tell me anything about it? Naturally I went to see Sam as soon as I got his letter, but he couldn't make sense of it no more than I could.' Pete could imagine them. 'You know Sybil is here with the children. I just told her our Pete had gone to Scotland, after all, instead of Germany, to be with his Dad, but I could see she thought it was a bit funny. Did he tell you he was coming? I'll be glad when you get home. The raspberries have come lovely this year, I'll have a pie for you Saturday. Love Mary. P.S. Give Pete my love and tell him I got his letter all right, and the card. I went to see his head teacher who said Pete had got into some trouble at school, but I was too worried to pay much heed to that. Pete will have to tell us all about it.'

Pete handed the letter back. 'Give Pete my love.' It would be all right, then, in the end, but there'd be a bit of a fuss first. Poor old Auntie Sybil, clucking like a hen round her own children. And poor Uncle Sam. He can say what he likes, though, thought Pete, if it makes him feel any better. He's only an uncle when all's said and done. It was his dad that mattered, not any uncles, not any more.

Mr Jenkins looked at his watch. 'Time we went along to the canteen,' he said. 'Next time you come and stay with me we'd better tell your mother first, and do it all proper and above-board.'

There was something Pete hadn't told him yet. 'Next year,' he said, 'A.R.C.S. have got a contract building a new road near Aberafon. Mr Coates told me this afternoon.'

'That so?' said Mr Jenkins.

'Truly,' said Pete. 'He told me to tell you. He'd only just heard today himself. You'll be able to live at home.'

Mr Jenkins stood looking out from his caravan steps over the reed-fringed loch for a long time. 'Be a bit of all right, that will,' he said at last.